$2 Yard sale
7-8-07

MW01168676

PRINCES & TOADS

Men Worth Keeping ... Men to Throw Away

SHARON TOBLER, Ph.D.

© 2000 Sharon Tobler

PERIWINKLE
PRESS

DEDICATION

To all my clients without whom
I could not have written this book.

ACKNOWLEDGMENTS

It is with reverence that I express my gratitude to all the players who have made this book possible. Each person has had a special and necessary role in its creation and production.

I would like to begin by acknowledging my preliminary readers: JJ Cochrane, who helped me to recognize that this manual was far more extensive than a "how to find your man" guide; and Palmer McGee, who inspired me to continue with my drafts when the order of the book was still in disarray.

In my search for a "mental health reader" who would inspect the manuscript to be sure all of my nuggets were theoretically sound, I could not think of someone I would trust more completely to do the job, eruditely, than my former doctoral advisor, Mary Ann Hoffman, Ph.D. Despite her extraordinary schedule, she graciously accepted my request. I continue to be touched by her generosity of time as well as her unwavering encouragement and support.

I feel blessed to have encountered Carol Harker, who is exceptional at her profession as editor. In spite of a packed schedule she gladly agreed to revise this manuscript.

I am indebted to Kathy Franklin, M.S.W., who gave her precious time to muse with me about questions I had regarding certain nuggets.

My artist, Ron Sebring, stretched himself far beyond his original agreement to help put in art form, my ideas for the book cover. I am indebted to him for his meticulous work, as well as his creativity which resulted in a design of unique splendor. I also want to thank his wife, Connie Sebring, who tirelessly and enthusiastically helped with *whatever* needed to be done. Nothing was ever too much to ask.

I am deeply appreciative of Lisa Nafziger, whose expert marketing guidance opened my eyes in the publishing world.

I am especially indebted to Marilyn Carlson for her involvement in cover selection, final proofing, and valuable assistance in marketing this project.

I wish to thank my brother, and his wife, who extended their support by consistently expressing the conviction that I would flourish with my project.

I cannot adequately express the gratitude I feel for my mother, who believed in me from the moment I told her I wanted to dedicate a portion of my career to writing. No matter how discouraged I got, *her* confidence that I would succeed always helped lift me from trepidation.

My father's modeling of ambition and work ethic have been instrumental. Without that influence, I am not sure this project would have been completed.

I am deeply indebted to my late ex-husband, who provided me with years of adventures and challenges in a marriage relationship. I do not believe I could have proficiently written this guide without those experiences.

Finally, my very deepest gratitude goes to "my two angels," Linda Smith and Bruce Carlson, without whom this manuscript would not have been in existence.

Linda told me the first day we met that this guide needed to be completed. She then stuck with me draft after draft, diligently reading and gently offering feedback. She encouraged me on blue days, laughed with me on bright days, and reassured me on doubtful days.

Bruce, "The Big Cheese," guaranteed me, in between shared belly laughs, that hot pink neon mistakes would litter this guide and that terror was part of the writing game. He *literally* made sure this work got published by using his wisdom, years of experience, clout, contacts, elbow grease, and much of his invaluable time to pull all the pieces of this project together.

I will not close until I have saluted the island on which I am blessed to live. Her exquisite beauty and radiance has enveloped me, providing the safe harbor for my creativity to "give birth" to this manuscript.

CONTENTS

INTRODUCTION

HOW TO USE THIS GUIDE

INTRODUCTION

This manual was created for women of all ages who are interested in finding and maintaining a healthy and loving relationship with a man.

I chose to call the male player "the Prince" or "the Toad," because both genders grew up reading the same fairy tales. "The Toad" was the undesirable male. "The Prince" was in hot demand because if you captured him you were destined to live "happily ever after."

The "Keeper ... Throwaway" concept was borrowed from the sport of fishing in which the "Catch" is *literally* measured to determine whether or not he is a "Keeper." In this guide, I have attempted when possible to help you "measure" your prospective Prince. I have taken a "hard-line" approach with my recommendations, meaning that I am quicker to "rule out," (Throw Away) than to "rule in," (Keep) when there is a doubt regarding whether the prospective Prince is a "Keeper."

I have four convictions regarding healthy and loving relationships:

1. That in order to have a healthy and loving relationship with another, you must FIRST have one with yourself.

2. That it is YOUR responsibility to no longer be *ruled* by your childhood experiences.

3. That YOU teach people how to treat you.

4. That you have at your command AT ALL TIMES your inner voice. She is far wiser than any guidebook. She has your answers. All you have to do is learn to LISTEN and TRUST her. (I realize this is *no* easy feat!)

HOW TO USE THIS GUIDE

This reference book is intended to succinctly and pointedly help you distinguish "Toads" from "Princes," as well as to answer questions regarding search, selection, and maintenance of the relationship.

There is no need to read this guide in sequence. Each page contains individual nuggets.

You may read casually or focus on the section that pertains to you.

Certain issues are readdressed from a different perspective.

If you decide to proceed from beginning to end, you will encounter a sequence ranging from the self-improvement necessary for a healthy and loving relationship, to keeping the marriage viable.

Since many of the issues paramount in self-love are equally important in a marriage, I have a somewhat random placement of topics. The progression of a relationship from its inception to marriage is never in any exact order, nor is it clear-cut or delineated. Consider this guide as a representation of this process.

This handbook addresses *numerous* relationship issues, as well as many of the "warning bells." It is *impossible*, however, to cover all the challenges and concerns involved in search, selection, and/or maintenance of the relationship.

The Exercise section is designed for those of you who wish to go beyond an intellectual understanding of the nuggets.

As a psychologist, I could not resist including a section on guidelines for seeking professional help.

Do not get discouraged ... relationships are difficult ... and mastering them takes TIME and ELBOW GREASE. Practice the nuggets that speak to you, and you WILL see results!

GETTING PREPARED:

Self-Improvement

Before ... you can experience a healthy and loving relationship with another you must FIRST have one with yourself.

For those of you ... who are not there yet, this section is provided to help you get started.

It is important ... that you concentrate on learning to love yourself *before* you begin the Hunt, since your "level" of self-love is directly related to your selection of partners. In other words, the more you love yourself, the greater the probability you will choose a partner who loves himself, and who will be capable of loving you.

Since the adventure ... you are preparing for is one of the most important trips you will ever take, I recommend buying a luxurious and expensive journal. One that will make your heart smile each time you pick it up. You will use this journal for homework exercises, thoughts, feelings, reflections, and any other entries that are relevant to your progress.

Now ... Let yourself unfold!

And remember ... There is NO quick fix in the realm of preparing yourself for a healthy and loving relationship with yourself or another.

LOVE and SELF-LOVE

There are *many* definitions of Love.... M. Scott Peck's definition, which is found in his best-seller **The Road Less Traveled** is:

the will to extend one's self for the purpose of nurturing one's own or another's spiritual growth

In this interpretation there is an emphasis on the importance of loving the Self *as much as* the Other, and loving the Other *as much as* the Self. Real Love spawns from being *equally* invested in the self and the other with regard to growth, satisfaction, safety, and security. Loving the self (or the other) may mean personal suffering and/or edging out of one's own emotional, physical, or spiritual comfort zone. Personal suffering, however, as well as stretching out of one's comfort zone, generates *self-* transformation. When each person is practicing this description of love, the love becomes cyclical, and each act of love enhances the next. The love expands.

Peck's use of the term "will" is another important feature of this definition, since this word infers "action." If one loves but refuses to "act" on the feeling, the result is that there is *no* nurturing of one's *own* or *another's* spiritual growth. The "felt" result is that there is no love.

"Spiritual" is a loosely used "New Age" buzzword. For purposes of *this* guide, the meaning of "spiritual" is "pure or transcendent, all-encompassing, exceeding and rising above any other form of growth." The term is *not* being used synonymously with "religious." One may be spiritual and not religious, religious and not spiritual, neither or both.

Having a loving and healthy relationship ... with yourself and with another requires priority.

It really is true that you won't love or be loved ... until you love yourself.

The most important person to love ... is yourself!

Self Love is ... applying M. Scott Peck's definition of **love** to yourself.

When you love yourself, you respect yourself.... You will not accept disrespect from your candidate.

When you love and respect yourself ... you are qualified to be a better partner.

When you love and respect yourself ... you know how you deserve to be treated and are capable of teaching your prospect how to treat you.

You will have significantly more respect for yourself ... if you resist becoming involved with someone you *know* will not be good for you.

Integrity is vital ... when it comes to loving yourself or loving another.

How do I develop Self-Love? ... By setting baby-step self-love goals and deciding to accomplish them. I cannot emphasize enough that starting with *attainable* goals is paramount since the key to the development of self-love is the *successful* accomplishment of these goals. (See exercise section.)

When you achieve one of your self-love goals ... hang out with your success for a while. Delight in it. Don't be in such a hurry to accomplish the next one.

Mindfulness, Courage, and Discipline ... are essential behaviors in the realm of acquiring self-love (and succeeding in a healthy and loving relationship).

The Self-Love journey is an arduous one.... Patience, Perseverance, and Practice are equally important commodities to exercise on this path.

Self-Love and Narcissism ... are *not* synonymous concepts. Narcissism is a mental disorder in which the sufferer lacks the ability to experience empathy and is wholly and totally self absorbed, often to the point of exploitation of others (in this case you), in order to achieve his own ends. He expects constant admiration and attention. He feels absolutely entitled. These features are *not* conducive to the establishment of a healthy and loving relationship. Yet, most women have at some point in their lives "fallen in love" with a narcissist, since many of them are quite charming, charismatic, and exciting.

Don't be a woman who makes a career of "falling in love" with narcissists.... As long as you are in love with one, you will *not* be happy.

You are *significantly* more likely to pick a Toad ... if you do NOT love yourself. Human nature dictates attraction to what is familiar. So, if "familiar" is self-loathing, you are doomed to repeat this pattern in the relationship. You will select a man who will treat you the way you are used to treating yourself. You will pick what you think you deserve. If you do not love yourself, how can you expect your Prince to love you?

How *capable* you are to treasure Your Prince ... is *equal* to the amount you treasure yourself.

Wholeness is developed through the attainment of Self-Love ... NOT through "conquest" of the Prince.

A clue as to whether you are "hole" or "whole": ... Generally speaking, if you hear yourself saying you *need* a man, you are "hole," and if you hear yourself saying you *want (desire)* a man, you are "whole."

In the realm of romantic relationships ... two halves equal two halves.

Hearts have to be open to be broken.... Cherish your broken heart and be grateful that you have had the experience.

You cannot fully love ... if your heart has never been exposed enough to be crushed.

The more your heart has loved and lost ... the better she loves.

SINGLEHOOD

Singlehood is NOT a second-class position.... Singlehood and Marriagehood are not comparable "states." They are simply different life paths. Each trek will offer some life lessons that will *not* be available on the other one. Your attitude *will* affect your experiences, so if you believe that you are a "second class" citizen because you are single, you will feel like one and your prospective Princes will pick that up on "their radar."

Singlehood offers an excellent opportunity ... to discover who you really are (outside of your roles as daughter, mother, wife, etc.).

You would not be reading this book if you were not interested in finding your Prince.... A *desire* to be connected with a man in a primary way is healthy. This desire becomes problematic, however, if you become consumed by the wish. "Obsession" severely limits options when it comes to selecting a partner with whom you may engage in a healthy and loving relationship.

When you are *ruled* by the desire to be in a relationship ... it is easy to overlook the road signs indicating that you are on a path of self-destruction. The "desperate" person will often "put up" with interactions in the relationship that are demeaning. At the very least, "settling" is a strong probability. Since life is so precious, and your time on the planet so short, do you not deserve to maximize the experience?

WORD CHOICES

Words empower and "dis"empower.... Become conscious of the words you use. Remove those that lessen your internal strength and use those that empower you.

Delete "try," "can't," and "should" from your vocabulary! Allowing these words to stay in your repertoire diminishes responsibility for your actions. Instead of "try," say "work on, or commit." "Try" permits "wiggle room" that is not constructive for personal growth. Instead of "can't," say "won't." "Can't" renders you the victim. Instead of "should," say "want" or "don't want." "Should" indicates that you are operating by *somebody else's*, rather than your own, standards.

"Don't" is a word that most people react negatively to ... because the "request" is usually a controlling demand. Instead of saying "don't," explain your wishes and invite him to do the same. It is not acceptable for him to say "don't" to you either.

Say, "allow" more often.... This word brings the power and responsibility back to you ... where it belongs! Notice how differently you feel when you say: "he takes me for granted" versus "I *allow* him to take me for granted."

AWARENESS

Awareness is a golden key ... used to unlock and free the true self. The true self is the only self capable of creating and maintaining a loving and healthy relationship.

Awareness promotes choice over behaviors.... Once you become aware of something, you have a choice about what to do about it.

Awareness *without* behavior change ... will *not* remedy the problem.

Be aware that your greatest assets are also your greatest liabilities.... For example, if you are extremely generous, you will surely be taken advantage of. Strive to hold on to your assets while not letting them slip into the liability arena.

His greatest assets are also his greatest liabilities.... Don't be surprised if what you are most drawn to at the beginning of the courtship, becomes one of the larger challenges as the relationship progresses. For example, you may have hungered for attention from a man and what you loved most was that he always made you his priority. You continue to be his priority. It is difficult to get any time or space to yourself. You are *still* the center of his universe and now, you are beginning to feel like you can't breathe!

The truth will set you free ... but, first, it may make you miserable!

Not knowing what you are doing ... does *not* keep you out of trouble. "Ignorance is *not* bliss."

You cannot change attitudes or behaviors ... until you are able to acknowledge that you have attitudes and/or behaviors to change.

Your motivation must be high if you wish to change "unwanted" attitudes and/or behaviors.... The longer you have had "bad habits," the harder they are to change.

Change your attitudes and your behaviors change.... Change your behaviors and your attitudes change!

Change your terminology and your attitudes *and* behaviors change.... Words are important messengers that reveal *your* mental, physical, and spiritual state to yourself and to others. Listen carefully to what you and others say. You will learn a lot about whomever you are listening to.

Insight regarding Family of Origin history holds many of the keys ... that unlock adult quandaries regarding feelings, thoughts, attitudes, values, and behaviors.

FAMILY OF ORIGIN

Family of Origin *does* dramatically affect every aspect of your life.... It does not mean, however, that you need to be *ruled* by your family of origin history.

It is *your* responsibility to reprogram your "adult-self" ... such that you are no longer governed by your childhood experiences.

Boundary behavior is taught in Family of Origin.... See "Boundaries," Keeper Dating section.

Family of Origin history has a dramatic influence on your choice of partner as well as your interactions with him.... It is advisable to experience a period of self-exploration *before* beginning the Hunt. Generally, the more you have worked through and let go of "old baggage" (childhood wishes, expectations, hopes, and wounds) the "healthier" your choice of partner and the healthier your interactions with him.

"Automatic pilot" means ... we act/think/feel in *programmed* ways based on what was taught to us in our family of origin. Gaining insight with regard to Family of Origin history allows for the opportunity to shift into "manual." Shifting into manual means that we can *decide* what actions, thoughts, and feelings fit into our true nature, and which do not. Those actions, thoughts, and feelings that we choose to keep become our own for which we are *responsible*. The others are discarded. Being in the position of "manual" greatly enhances the probability of having a healthy and loving relationship. It is heartening to discover that we do *not* need to be bound by family of origin programming. We can learn, choose, and change!

Your "automatic" reflex will be to see *his* behaviors and intentions through *your* "family of origin lenses." ... He is not a member of your family of origin. You are *not* required to respond as though he is your parent. Put yourself into "manual" and negotiate, as an adult, the issue at hand. (See previous nugget, "Automatic Pilot," for explanation of "manual.")

How do I heal my childhood wounds? ... In two overlapping stages: "insight" and "action." First you need to discover what the wounds are, and how they have been interfering with your ability to love yourself and another. Then you need to make a decision. Do you *desire* to "fix" those behaviors and attitudes which you smartly acquired as a child to "survive" those hurts and threats, but which are now hindering your growth? Or do you remain in your "victim" position; the position that was bestowed upon you when you were a child and powerless to act on your own behalf? Gaining "insight" alone will not heal the wounds. It takes courage, hard work, patience, perseverance, and lots of practice to walk through the "action" stage. Those who choose to immerse themselves in this stage have my admiration. (See exercise section.)

The deeper you dive into BOTH "insight and action" ... the greater the potential for a healthy and loving relationship.

Your parents were assigned the role of "caretaker and provider" ... NOT your Prince. If you do your psychological homework *before* the Hunt, you are less likely to confuse the cast of characters.

A purpose for "revisiting" the past is ... to prevent "automatic pilot" in the present and the future.

A purpose for "revisiting" the past is ... to eradicate the tape that plays the *same* self-destructive story over and over again and install a new tape which will promote a healthier and more loving existence.

A purpose for "revisiting" the past is ... to ease the *pain* associated with the traumas, so that they lose their power and simply become a part of your history rather than remaining in your psyche as highly charged emotional experiences. Lessening the power and mitigating the pain of the traumas is accomplished by "revisiting" the incidents accompanied by the two "parts" of yourself : the "parent" of your inner child, and your "inner child." The "parent" provides safety and protection by attending the events with the child as she "relives and repairs" the feelings associated with the traumas. There are many ways to "repair the damage." (See exercise section.)

It is NOT necessary to "revisit" *all* the old wounds ... in order to heal.

One does NOT "revisit" the past ... in order to blame the primary caregivers who made the mistakes.

Many avoid "revisiting" the past ... because they fear the pain. The problem is that the dysfunctional behaviors that are developed in order to *escape* the pain are often more stressful than the original traumas.

You will be significantly less attracted to Toads ... if you mend your childhood wounds.

The anticipatory anxiety is almost always worse ... than the feared object/experience.

If your history is one in which you go from one chaotic and destructive relationship to the next ... it is likely that your family of origin was also bedlam. You are repeating the pattern because you have not successfully healed old wounds. Pandemonium seeking can be addictive. If you suspect that you are addicted to tumultuous relationships, consider pursuing professional help, since addictions can be so devastating.

DARK SIDE

All human beings *do* own a dark side.... Do not be frightened by it.

The goal is to embrace your dark side ... not obliterate it. The only way you will succeed in "bettering" your always imperfect self is to take responsibility *without judgment* for *all* the parts of yourself. Obviously, for most, the shadow is the area hardest to acknowledge. However, when it is not accepted it interferes with self-growth and healthy relationships.

It is the "demons" inside us that we do *not* know, that are the dangerous ones ... not the ones we know. The ones we know we can learn to manage.

Recognizing a "demon" does not mean you will act on it.... You may discover that you want to sleep with your best friend's husband. Knowing that about yourself does not make you "bad," it simply makes you human. He may be a very attractive man. What you *do* have control over is what you will *do* with this realization.

GUILT and SHAME ... JOY and PAIN

Guilt is a "wasted" emotion.... Nothing growth-enhancing comes from the experience of this sentiment. Adult decisions need to be driven by conscience, not guilt. Holding on to guilt has the potential to cause you physical, emotional, and spiritual harm. (See exercise section.)

Shame deserves separate mention.... This sensation is an experience that all of us know and loathe. It often occurs after a "burst of healthy grandiosity." For instance you may work up the nerve to tell your Prince that you love him for the first time and his response is to ignore what you just said or to tactlessly tell you that he does not love you in return. Another scenario would be expressing an interest in the use of a sex toy during a sexual encounter and being met with a response that infers that he sees you as "perverted" or "dirty." You want to crawl in a hole and never come out again. Like depression, shame is an unexpressed feeling turned inward. It has the capacity to destroy wherever it lodges itself, whether it be in your mind, body, or spirit. It is imperative that it be expelled. You did *not* cause it, but *only* you may exorcise (release) it. If you are unsuccessful in doing so, seek professional help.

The terms "shame and guilt" are often used synonymously.... They are *not* the same. Shame is more dangerous to the Self. Shame has penetrated into your cells and your psyche. It is far more difficult to release.

Do you feel guilt or shame? ... Generally when you feel guilt, although you may be afraid to confess what you feel guilty about, there is a desire to do it. When you feel shame, you do *not* want to confess it. You want to hide. You feel unacceptable to the core. Shame is a part of you. Guilt is an action, feeling, or thought committed.

Joy and Pain are intimately related.... You can only feel as high (joy) as you can feel low (pain/misery/despair/suffering). The greater your capacity to feel joy, the more profound will be your experience of pain. Imagine a horizontal baseline crossed by an infinitely high and infinitely low vertical bar. The baseline is labeled "comfortably numb." How high you can climb up the bar toward joy is equal to how low you descend in despair.

It is a gift to have the capacity to experience these intense feelings (joy and pain) ... since there is no greater experience on the planet than FEELING alive.

Numbness inhibits FEELING alive.... You become numb to dull or escape excruciating pain. The problem is that numbness also blunts joy.

REJECTION

Since rejection is a part of life ... learning how to survive it is actually good for you. Do not confuse rejection, however, with a compromise of self.

How to respectfully and tactfully reject others ... is an art worth learning . Mastering this skill will enable you to travel with considerably more freedom and ease in the world since you will feel more adept at guarding your boundaries. (See exercise section.)

Disappointment and grief ... are additional "afflictions" of the dating world (and life in general). Learning how to deal with them are valuable life lessons. When either of these occur, view them as opportunities for personal growth. Also remember that you were thriving BEFORE you met him; you will learn to thrive again.... You just need time.

Pain is a great teacher.... Do not be afraid of it. We learn our greatest life lessons and experience our finest spurts of spiritual growth as a result of pain.

There is enough pain that visits all of us without our *inviting* **more....** Why willingly engage in situations in which it is obvious from the "get go" that there will be agony to withstand? Women are chronically guilty of entering into "bad" romantic relationships knowing full well that the path will be littered with disappointments, betrayals, and sorrows. Decide to relinquish your temptations to enter into a liaison with an obvious Toad. It will improve your self-love status!

LETTING GO

Mastering the art of "letting go" is a valuable life lesson ... since you will be obligated to do so over and over again. The ability to "let go" of who and/or what was in the past provides s p a c e for who and/or what is in the present. Although one never enjoys "letting go," knowing you have the skill will effectively ease the search for the Prince and/or maintenance of the relationship. If you are having difficulty letting go of a relationship, be sure to do the "letting go" exercise. (See exercise section.)

You will not succeed in a healthy and loving bond ... if you have not resolved and let go of your past relationships.

A letting go "rule of thumb": ... allow yourself approximately one month of grieving for each year of involvement.

It is ideal to enter into a new relationship healed from all previous ones.... Healing takes time. If you insist on dating before you have "recovered" from your previous relationship, date casually and go out with more than one man at a time. Dating more than one man at a time lessens the chances of "reinvolving" yourself too soon. You are vulnerable and not very capable of making smart choices when you are freshly "released" from a relationship. If you get back to the serious stuff before you are ready, you risk finding yourself in a rebound situation and since most rebounds end up in the "trash" heap, not only are you grieving the loss of the previous relationship, but you now have a second relationship to end.

Many rebound relationships ... are fantasy relationships and consequently even more difficult and painful to terminate than the previous relationship. (A "fantasy" is always more difficult to give up than a "reality.")

It is essential to keep "current" in all your relationships (past and present).... In present relationships this means that on a daily basis you are saying and doing all that needs to be said and done. One way to monitor whether you are accomplishing this challenging task is to ask yourself whether you would have said and done everything you wanted to say and do if that person were to drop dead tomorrow. Regarding past relationships, ask yourself the same question. Keeping relationships current is important for two reasons: it urges you to live in the present, which is all you really have, and it guards against the unexpected. If a sudden death should occur, you are not riddled with regret, *in addition* to grief.

When you feel him slipping away ... Let Him Go! You will save yourself a lot of unnecessary pain and frustration if you let him go rather than persuading him to stay. Of greater significance, groveling compromises your self-love and respect.

DEPENDENCY

You do not "love" someone when you believe you cannot live without him.... You are *dependent* on him.

Being in a relationship does *not* guarantee security.... Even if you are in a good relationship with no considerations of ever terminating it, a sudden death could leave you alone in an instant. Security comes from within, *not* from being connected to someone else.

Being "attached" and being "bonded" are not the same....
When you are attached, you are parasitic. You believe that you
need your partner to survive. When you are bonded, the essence
of the connection is one of mutuality and equality. You desire
your partner but do *not* perceive that you *need* him to survive.

It is natural to *desire* being taken care of.... It is a problem
when those desires *rule* your life.

**It is YOUR problem if you are *depending* on him to make
you feel good about yourself....** The only person who has the
ability to make you feel good about yourself is YOU! When you
experience that he has "made you feel good about yourself,"
what has really happened is that you have *allowed* him to touch
that place inside you that knows how to "feel good." You have
given him the power to contact that place. Take the power back
and recognize that you can only feel those good feelings inside
you if they are there to begin with. He does *not* "put" those
feelings inside you. The converse is also true. He can only make
you feel bad about yourself if you *allow* him to do it.

**Looking "outside" of yourself for what may only be
discovered "inside" is a dead-end road....** Fairy tales live in
our hearts, generation after generation, because it is easier to
believe that the Prince (outside) will heal all hurts, make you
whole, and relegate your life to a state of serenity and peace,
than it is to walk the long and rocky road (inside) of discovery,
healing, forgiving, and acquiring self-love. Fairy tales inhibit
self-growth.

ALONE versus LONELY

Being alone and feeling lonely are NOT synonymous experiences.... When you are alone your heart is happy. When you are lonely, your heart is sad and sometimes afraid.

Words that evoke the experience of lonely: ... isolated, alienated, detached, forlorn, scared, sad.

Words that evoke the experience of alone: ... solitude, whole, complete, renewed, calm, peaceful, creative, exhilarated.

It is not uncommon to feel lonely in a relationship.... Many people believe the solution to loneliness is to be in a relationship. Those of you who have been lonely and married, with children, know this is far from the truth!

Being lonely is really an alienation from yourself ... *not* the result of "lacking the company" of others. Feeling lonely is a sign that you are not enjoying your *own* company.

It is not unusual to experience loneliness as a constant companion ... when you do not love yourself. Whether you are married or not, whether you have children or not, you will feel lonely. The solution: get going on your self-love work.

Enjoying being alone does not mean you are immune from occasional bouts of loneliness.... However, when you have a good relationship with yourself, you know how to "walk through the feelings" without overwhelming sadness or fear. You may decide to take a walk, paying particular attention to the smells in the air. You might watch a dog playing with a ball or a bird making a nest. You might contact an acquaintance and suggest a movie, or just have a nice conversation on the phone with a friend. The feelings *will* pass.

Paradoxically, learning to enjoy being alone ... improves togetherness.

Learn to thrive *without* having your focus be on the Prince.... Remember how easy it is to "lose yourself" in the relationship when you put all your energy into him?

If you have a history of extensive dating and/or "always having a man in your life" ... you may want to make a deliberate choice to stop dating for a while. This will give you a chance to get your priorities in order as well as to experience "being alone." Learning to enjoy your aloneness and mastering the art of self-reliance will significantly improve your future partnership along with your self-love.

Learn to enjoy your own company.... You truly are your own best friend. You are the only one who was with you when you were born, has been with you through EVERY life experience, and will be with you when you die. Everyone else in your life comes and goes. If you do not enjoy your own company, you risk conveying this to your prospect. He may then begin to wonder why *he* derives pleasure from you. When you do not delight in your own company, it is easy to transmit a message which pleads "neediness and dependency." Many "good men" will run if that is what they detect. Toads are often drawn to neediness and dependency because it offers a "playing field" for potential abuse and neglect.

VICTIM versus VICTOR

Are you "acting" like a victim? ... Many women have never asked themselves this question. Early female life programming typically does not emphasize learning to "take charge" (as is taught to males), so it is not uncommon for some women to "automatically" allow their men to take over the control of their lives where their parents left off.

The definition of victim, simply put, ... is that someone else is "managing" YOUR life.

Remember how you felt as a kid when you couldn't have your way? ... That is the visceral sensation of being "managed."

A child *is* a victim.... Someone else *does* control her life.

When you are chronologically an adult and living as a victim ... no matter how much it doesn't *feel* like a choice, you actually are *allowing* someone else to "manage your life." There are some exceptions (certain physical or mental disabilities) in which you truly *are* incapable of caring for yourself. When this is the case, you hold "child status."

Living the "victim lifestyle" may be easier than living the life of victor.... Decisions are made by others. The victim is not responsible or accountable if/when something goes awry. The victim does not bear consequences for "bad actions or choices."

The price the victim pays is ... freedom of choice.

Having freedom of choice ... may be so scary that you opt for the "lifestyle of victim." At the very least, make your decision consciously.

If these phrases are part of your vocabulary when referring to yourself, you may be living as a victim:
- My destiny is controlled by another
- I feel like a child
- It is someone else's fault
- It is someone else's problem
- Someone else is responsible for
- I am unaccountable
- I am powerless
- I am in prison
- I am scared, but do not exert the **courage** to act

You are most likely living as a victor when you use these phrases about yourself:
- I am in control of my own destiny
- I am a mature adult
- It is my fault
- It is my problem
- I am responsible for
- I am accountable
- I am powerful
- I am free
- I am scared, but I act **courageously**

COURAGE

The definition of courage: ... acting *in spite* of the fear. If the behavior is not feared, it is not an act of courage. For example, riding elevators is not generally an act of courage; however, for an elevator phobic, riding one is an act of great courage.

Courage is a gift.... Work to get it. When you know you have it, you may venture into "risksville." On your deathbed, you will have far less to regret.

Gaining courage *does not* mean "throwing caution to the wind." ... What is most important to keep in mind when exercising your courage is whether you are caring for yourself in a loving and healthy way. There may be times when the courageous thing to do is *not* act.

FILLING UP

The truth is ... that the *only* person who is capable of making you happy (and "filling you up") is YOU.

Nature plagues us with a *simultaneous* fear of abandonment and engulfment.... In a state of abandonment, you are utterly alone. In a state of engulfment, you exist no more. To lessen this fear, strive toward wholeness. When you do *not* feel whole, you believe that you *need* others to literally survive. This *need* to keep others appeased in order to avoid being swallowed up or abandoned, prevents you from setting limits and from being your true self. When you feel whole, you *desire* but do not *need* others to stay alive. You feel safe enough to set limits and to be your true self because you are less paralyzed by the prospect of being engulfed or abandoned.

You are *not* an empty vessel waiting for him to fill you up.... It is up to YOU to supply your needs. He cannot replenish the void even if he does love you. Those unrealistic expectations that you hold for him are really childhood wounds that need repairing and healing.

Many women are taught to put themselves last, especially when it comes to simultaneous wishes.... This is a lesson that needs to be relearned! Remember what the flight attendant instructs just before "takeoff" regarding the management of oxygen masks if they are dropped for use? The attendant tells the passengers to *first* put the masks on themselves, *then* help a child or any other person who is having difficulty putting it on.

The fact is that you cannot share your wealth until you have wealth to share.... No matter how devoted you may be to your role of "filling *others* up," if you are "empty" you have nothing to give.

The more you fill yourself up ... the more you have to give. (See exercise section.)

Sometimes "filling yourself up" means ... NOT meeting someone else's needs.

HEALTHY ROUTINES

Practice good health for the head, heart, groin, and spirit....
You are a unique being with a body and spirit unlike any other,
so treat yourself with the utmost care. Eat healthily, drink lots
of pure water, restrict your intake of chemicals, (caffeine,
alcohol, recreational drugs), and get plenty of sleep. Exercise on
a *regular* basis. Include a weight training program, as well as
muscle toning, stretching and/or yoga. Incorporate daily
meditation/ prayer/relaxation techniques, or quiet time, into
your schedule. Dedicate a few hours a week to "play " in which
the sole purpose is to have fun. Spend time with dear friends. (If
you don't have any, make it a priority to acquire a few.) Friends
and lovers supply different needs; they are not interchangeable.
Always practice safer sex. Sexually Transmitted Diseases may
be fatal. Attend to your mental health. Empirical scientific
studies have documented that poor mental health substantially
increases your risk of physical disease. Begin to discover your
spiritual self. If you have no idea who that is, initiate your
journey by reading some books on the subject. A greater
contact with your spiritual self may lead to more clarity and
curiosity about your life purpose.

Learning to relax ... is vital to your physical, emotional, and
spiritual health. Three methods of relaxation often used are:
diaphragm breathing, deep-muscle, and visualization. Reduced
levels of physical and mental agitation substantially improve
your overall well-being. It is impossible to be truly relaxed and
anxious at the same time. (See exercise section.)

Having at your disposal relaxation skill techniques ... is also
helpful in making the "hunt stage" run more smoothly. Meeting
a potential Prince will generate periods of acute anxiety.

Knowing that you have the capacity to reduce your panic will enable you to take more risks.

R & Rs are a necessity.... No matter how dedicated you are to your spiritual, emotional, and physical health, you WILL need time to "integrate" all your newly learned skills. During this period, rest and relax; don't attempt to learn or practice anything new.... Just sit.

Commit to moments of stillness.... In addition to providing integration time for those who need it, periods of stillness are often the moments in which greatest clarity abounds.

Be kind to yourself.... Your self-loathing thoughts and behaviors have taken a lifetime to acquire. You cannot change those patterns overnight. Allow yourself to "slip" gracefully. Pick yourself up, smile ... and start again. You WILL prevail!

"Being" and "doing" activities are both necessary requirements in order to succeed in a healthy and loving relationship with yourself (or with another).... "Being" activities have no purpose other than to spend time with your "core/inner/spirit self." "Being" activities provide an opportunity for integrating things that you are learning about yourself. Examples of "being" activities include: quiet time, prayer, meditation, a stroll on the beach, smelling roses, watching the rain glide down a window pane, making angels in the snow. "Being" activities may be extended into contacts with others who are concurrently in the same state. An example may be reading a bedtime story to your child in which you are totally "in the moment" with her, appreciating her beauty and feeling how much you love her. "Doing" activities range anywhere from running errands to dating to making a living. There is a distinct goal in the "doing" activity, and not a lot of time to synthesize. The "doing" activities, are life requirements; without them you cannot thrive. The self-love goal is to maintain a balance between these two genres of activities.

DECISIONS

Do not be afraid to make decisions.... They are life lessons.

You will learn something from each decision you make ... because decisions bear consequences. Anticipating and dealing with the *consequences* of a decision are the challenges (and life lessons), *not* whether or not to make the decision. Also keep in mind that NO decision is a decision.

You are expending much undue energy if you absorb yourself with regret regarding a decision made (or not made).... It will change nothing. What is done is done. Now get on with learning your lesson from the mistake.

Admit that you make mistakes.... Forgive yourself and work on not making the same one again.

FAILURES

There is no such thing as failure.... There are only *perceived* failures.

Remove the word "failure" from your vocabulary ... and instead say "opportunity".

The greatest life lessons are learned from ... *perceived* failures *when* they are viewed as OPPORTUNITIES.

You are afraid to fail because it hurts! ... "Opportunities" on the other hand, are exciting. Which would you rather feel?

A fear of failure ... often inhibits risk taking and immobilizes action. A fear of **success** can do the same. If you are not "moving" or "risk taking" check to see whether you are fearing the failure or the success ... or both!

A fear of success is usually more complicated ... because it is overdetermined, meaning that there is *more* than one reason for the distress. A common thread weaving through all the fear of success factors is a generalized anxiety of the unknown. An apprehension of change can also paralyze and impede action.

You are far more likely to succeed when you experience a "failure" as an "opportunity" ... because you are *enthusiastic* about an opportunity and *fear* failure. When you are *eager*, you are more likely to risk and to act. Being *fearful* causes you to be more hesitant to risk and to act.

You are not going to get what you want ... if you don't go after it! "God helps those who help themselves."

43

YOU ARE THE EXPERT

You **are the expert ...** not the author, doctor, lawyer, or Indian chief. It is natural to be drawn to the "easy path." We desire to have the most with the least amount of effort. We are extremely vulnerable when promised a quick fix. (The diet, drug, and cosmetic industries are living proof of that.) So when the expert promises the solution, we are sitting ducks.

How do you become your own expert? ... The technique involves no devices. Processing information through the human computer simply requires listening to your inner voice through body cues, images, and spontaneous words. If the data is a "match" the gut will say "ah ha!" It will *feel* right; there will be an inner knowing.

Experts are "transmitters of data." ... They do *not* have your answers.

Your inner voice has the answers.... You need to learn how to listen ... and trust her.

It is risky to follow the expert's advice without first ... running it through your "human" computer to determine whether the recommendation is a "fit." If you are one of the many women who was taught early in life to be a follower rather than a leader, when the data doesn't "compute" it is easy to conclude that you are the defective one. Usually when the data doesn't "match," it means that this expert is not "your expert" and would be better suited for someone else. (If you *never* find an expert who is in tune with your convictions, explore whether you are in some form of denial regarding your quest.)

Another reason that it is perilous to blindly follow the expert ... is that if the solution *does* work, you risk becoming dependent on the expert, ultimately undermining your self-confidence. In cults, the results of such tendencies are taken to the extreme.

Trust your body.... She knows only two sensations: comfort (pleasure) and discomfort (pain). (Comfort does *not* mean immediate "pleasure" gratification such as bingeing or giving into lust with a high-risk partner.) An example of "comfort and discomfort" would be noticing whether your body feels pleasure or pain when you think about spending the rest of your life with your partner. (Remember that pleasure and pain exist emotionally as well as physically.)

Call the experts, "coaches." ... This may help lessen their "authority" over you.

Discovering that *you* are the expert ... is both exciting and frightening.

There is never only one answer.... The avenues of solutions are limitless.

Sometimes the answer is not immediately clear.... Don't stress yourself looking for it. Just let it come to you in it's own time.

Stop going to everyone else for the answers to your questions. Listen to yourself ... then move your feet!

All "negative feelings" will have an impact on how accurately you can interpret your "gut." ... Since it is impossible to rid yourself of all "negative feelings," work on eliminating **anxiety**, and you will dramatically increase your ability to correctly read your intuition. ("Negative feelings" = **anxiety**; depression; unfulfilled childhood expectations, wishes, hopes, and dreams; emotional wounds; unforgiven acts; blame; resentment; hatred; doubt; self-loathing; and guilt.)

"Gut solutions" are often ignored, mistrusted, or even unheard in the Western World.... We rely on the brain. We are robbing ourselves of great wisdom when we refuse to counsel with our "sixth sense."

When you need to make a decision ... use your head *and* your "gut."

Listen to the opinions of others you trust, but let the final conclusion be your own.... In the end, you are the one who has to live with and be accountable for the decision.

It is very hard to hear your inner voice's "wisdom" if you don't put aside time to listen to her.... Some call it meditation or prayer, some call it "quiet uninterrupted time" or relaxation, some call it daydreaming.... It does not matter what you call it. What is important is that you commit to periods in which you do nothing but listen.

Trust the Universe.... Sometimes your inner voice "nags" you to act contrary to your "logical self." For example, you want children and you are married to someone who will most probably make a good father. Your logical self tells you to stay with him since he is a good man and your biological clock is running out. Yet, you *know* that he is not the man with whom you want to spend the rest of your life. It is at these times that you *need* to trust that acting on your intuition will bring you to your "higher good." If another person's life will be affected by your action (such as in this example), you need to trust that acting on your intuition will bring him to his "higher good" as well.

Don't ignore thoughts, feelings, or actions that nag or bother you.... Your "gut" is signaling you.

THE HUNT

This is the phase ... in which you are meeting prospective Princes and collecting data to eventually determine whether you have a "Keeper."

BEFORE YOU BEGIN THE HUNT

Before you begin the Hunt ... complete the ABCs, Pre-date Checklist, Ten Essential Characteristics, and Ideal Partnership Exercises. (See exercise section.)

Relationships are challenging! ... If you do not have the **time, energy**, and/or **inclination** to work on a relationship, don't get into one!

TIPS

You are not going to meet the Prince ... if you stay at home! (See exercise section.)

From the moment you meet your date: BE YOURSELF! ... If he doesn't like who that is, move on to your next candidate.

STAY AWAKE! ... All the clues are present regarding whether he is a Prince right from the *beginning* of the courtship.

It is vital to stay awake at EVERY stage of the relationship.... Otherwise, it will crash.

Don't let yourself get so absorbed with the relationship ... that you no longer know the difference between fantasy and reality, love and lust, loneliness and hunger.

It really is OK to ask him out.... If he doesn't think it is ... move on!

Some of you who have been married and/or are more chronologically mature ... may choose not to "date around," since you have had your period of experimentation and/or know exactly what you are looking for. Spend your valuable time doing the "getting prepared" homework, and when you are ready, use the more likely ways (through friends and becoming involved in activities which you enjoy), to meet serious candidates.

For those of you who have not dated extensively ... take the time, even with candidates who obviously are not "Prince material." Each rendezvous will be a good "learning experience."

Do things you've never done, try things you've never tried, go places you've never gone.... You will be proud of your successes, and you may meet the Prince. If you don't meet him, you could meet someone who will lead you to him.

Beware of Newspaper Personals ... they are a breeding ground for lies.

Beware of "Cyberchemistry" ... it is usually not REAL chemistry.

Beware of extremely strong sexual chemistry.... You are either in for extraordinary healing or extraordinary pain since this person is probably an "updated version" of your childhood caretakers. Most of the time these highly charged relationships fail since the participants are unaware of the underground currents that are driving the attraction.

We all know that Bars are "meat markets." ... Only go there if you are looking for "meat!"

If he is a "hunk" ... he may be more interested in devoting his time to what he *looks* like than who he *is*. If you are simply interested in a man to "show off," you will have met your goal. If you want a man of substance, pay special attention to what he has developed "inside."

Generally speaking, "bad boys" and "boy toys" make great dates ... but not great mates.

Opposites attract; however, "like kinds" generally make better long-term bedmates.... The more you naturally have in common (ethnic background, education, socioeconomic class, family history, values), the less you will need to overcome.

MEETING MEN

An excellent way to meet "like men"... is to alert your male and female friends, coworkers, and even family members that you are ready to meet prospects. Let them do the screening for you.

Expect to find him in the most unlikely places.... Stay vigilant wherever you are since your Prince could be standing (or sitting) right next to you.

Go to places where you will find "like men." ... Become involved in things that interest you (athletics, politics, wildlife conservation ...). If you meet someone at one of these functions, you will have met a man who has a shared interest.

If you want to marry a lawyer ... go to the law library.

If you want to marry a doctor ... go to the medical library.

If you want to marry an outdoors man ... go white-water rafting!

Enroll yourself in a class of interest at a university.... This is another way to meet a man with whom you have something in common.

Take an auto mechanics or bicycle repair class.... You are bound to be in the gender minority at this gathering.

Visit the home improvement stores ... even if you don't need to purchase anything. Men love to frequent these outlets.

Spend time at computer stores.... This is another "hot spot" for encountering men.

Line up behind attractive men ... when you are checking out at the grocery store and start a conversation.

KEY WORDS TO PONDER IN YOUR SEARCH

Trust - Respect - Responsibility - Commitment - Forgiveness - Tactful Honesty - Communication - Chemistry - Compatibility - Care - Courage - Consideration - Patience - Perseverance - Practice - Reliability.... Start right from the beginning to assess whether he values these concepts.

NO EXCUSES

Having had your heart broken in the past is not an excuse to avoid venturing out again.... It is important to have time alone after a breakup since proper grieving is necessary. However, we are social creatures and we heal by being in contact with others. Establishing a balance of time alone and time with others is the goal. The Prince is waiting.

You are not going to meet the Prince if you do not allow yourself to take risks.... Ask yourself, "will I SURVIVE if I am rejected?" Of course you will.... Nobody enjoys having a bruised ego, but your life will go on ... and you will learn something from the experience.

Gauge which emotional risks you will take and when you will take them.... Obviously, you do not want to tell your prospect on the first date that which you feel the most shame about. You do, however, want to begin venturing into emotional risk-taking early on, mostly because you want to see how he will react. Does he listen and encourage you to continue, or does he minimize and/or dismiss you?

You have had a successful first date. Above all, do not wait for his call.... You may give yourself a "con job" to justify staying at home to wait, but by the end of the day, you will be mad at him for not calling, afraid he will never call again, and upset with yourself because you did not get anything done. Sound familiar? Rest assured ... if he is the Prince he will call until he reaches you.

And ... Don't beat yourself up if he doesn't call again.... It simply was not meant to be.

Consider a "date from hell"... an experience and good practice. Do not let it divert you from your goal. Keep dating!

There is no perfect Prince.... Set priorities.... If he loves adventure flicks and you prefer drama, you will manage. If he is a womanizer, the relationship is probably not viable unless *he* is ready to do something about the problem.

If you are waiting for someone who has it all together ... you are waiting for Godot. (Remember, Mr. Godot never showed up.)

If you discover on the date that you don't know who "yourself" is ... practice being and doing what "feels" right. Don't try to figure it out. Just let your inner guide take you on the rendezvous. When you get home, do more "getting prepared" homework.... Then get back to dating!

If you find yourself attempting to let him know how "impressive" you are ... do more "getting prepared" homework.... Then hit the dating scene once again.

There are MANY Princes.... It is *not* true that only one Prince awaits each woman on "the Hunt." What *is* true is that when you are *really* ready to meet the Prince ... you will.

When you conclude that all the good Princes are either married or gay ... what you are *really* saying is that you are not *ready* to find your Prince.

DO'S & DONT'S

From the beginning ... your body cues [comfort (pleasure) and discomfort (pain)] will reveal at every juncture whether you are on the right path. Those body cues will continue to remain reliable throughout selection and maintenance of the relationship. All you need to do is pay attention.

Treat your date as you wish to be treated.... He deserves the same respect from you as you wish to receive from him.

It is permissible to give the prospective Prince a second chance ... but YOU are the fool if you give him a third.

Things are often NOT as they appear.... This truth "cuts" both ways.... He could be "a wolf in sheep's clothing," OR he could be the Prince wearing a public mask that does not initially attract you. For example, you will only marry a "Dockers" specimen, and this guy is wearing polyester. If your intuition is not screaming a "*dangerous* NO" ... give him a chance! It is often true that the men who do not initially appear as appealing turn out to be the "good" men. (Remember the "TIPS" nugget regarding "extremely strong sexual chemistry"? Those relationships usually fail.)

If you have made it abundantly clear that you are available and interested ... let him make the next move. If you are pursuing him at the beginning, this pattern will continue later on.

"Playing" hard to get ... is manipulative and dishonest.

Do NOT ... sacrifice ANY part of yourself to ANY man!

Never ... divulge more about yourself than you are comfortable revealing.

NEVER, EVER ... compromise your integrity. It will thwart your self love.

If he appears to be "too good to be true" ... he probably is.

Do not waste your valuable time ... on someone who is NOT interested in you.

Never "break a date" with a woman friend to go out with a man.... The message you are giving yourself is that finding a man (or being with a man) is more important than spending time with women friends. This is an example of a behavior that may foster an eventual "losing of the self" in relationship to a man.

Do not marry a Prince ... expecting that you can change him.

Do not believe him ... when he says "he will change for you."

You cannot decide to attend to the relationship "later." ... The only time you have is NOW. Yesterday is gone and tomorrow is iffy.

Don't settle! ... Many women are so grateful to have found a "good man" that they are willing to accept comfort and companionship as sufficient for the long haul. You deserve so much more. The possibilities are limitless. Take the risk, rock the boat, and unveil the mysteries that lie beneath the surface. If you discover that there are no intrigues, move on.

Do not make a "promise" that you cannot keep.... It will decrease trust in the relationship and diminish your self-love.

It is a waste of time to focus on your partner's defects.... Many of us *focus* on our partner's defects because it is much easier to do that than to focus on our own. Yet, it is only when *each* partner takes responsibility for his/her *own* defects that the relationship can move forward. Focusing on each other's flaws will only keep the relationship stuck.

Since "opposites" attract ... "act" like a child (irresponsible, impulsive, not worried about tomorrow) and you will most probably attract someone who "acts" like a parent (serious, no fun, controlling, too worried about tomorrow). The reverse is also true. "Act" like an adult (able to play, love, and work responsibly) and you will most likely attract another adult.

Never issue an ultimatum unless you are ready to follow through.... Remember what happened to the little boy who "cried wolf"?

Ultimatums are serious business ... and should *not* be considered until every other option has been explored.

Unacceptable behavior is just that ... unacceptable. Do not waste your time attempting to figure out whether you are "distorting" your opinion. If your *perception* is that his behavior is unacceptable ... it is! Do not let him (or anyone else) convince you otherwise. What you have to rely on is your inner voice, and if she deduces that you are being mistreated ... you are.

What he can and cannot "get away with" regarding his treatment of you ... is etched in granite by the time you reach the commitment stage. Set limits!

Abuse is NOT limited to physical hitting.... It includes emotional and verbal battery as well.

Abuse is abuse is abuse.... There is *no* condition under which you should "put up with it." GET OUT! The longer you stay in an abusive relationship, the harder it is to extricate yourself.

Married men are a disaster.... This is a waste of your precious time. In this triangle there is always waiting, and you are the one doing it. You spend the holidays alone; you cannot call him. The relationship is based on HIS schedule. He generally will not leave his wife to be with you, and if he does, he comes with a HUGE parcel of emotional baggage.

If you have a pattern ... of getting involved with married men you may need to do some more "getting prepared" homework to discover what you are hiding from or fearful about regarding enjoying an "available Prince."

HUMOR

Keep your humor.... Even though you are exploring options for a lifetime commitment, keep your ability to laugh at yourself.... Let's face it: the Hunt phase can be VERY funny.... Woody Allen has amassed a fortune by comically putting our life stories on the screen!

"KEEPER" DATING

"Keeper" dating means ... that you are dating him exclusively and investing your time and energy in this particular man to determine whether you have a "keeper." If you thought the early dating stage was hard ... this phase is even more challenging! There are many reasons for this. You are starting to get closer and you are becoming more invested in what he *really* thinks of you. It is also getting more difficult to hide your vulnerabilities. You are beginning to feel more exposed. You are seeing some of his flaws and have experienced a few disappointments. You may have encountered some minor conflicts. The newness of the sexual passion may have waned ever so slightly. The terror is setting in.... Can I commit to him? He is not as perfect as I had previously imagined.... Hold on ... the emotional roller coaster ride is just beginning ... and EVERYTHING you are feeling is part and parcel of this stage. In time, the roller coaster will slow down, come to a halt, and you will be able to get out. When you step out of the roller coaster, you will either be parting ways or setting a date for the BIG day.

TIME

Developing a meaningful and healthy relationship takes time.... You CANNOT hurry Mother Nature.

Time really is on your side.... The more slowly you progress in the relationship, the more reliable your data will be regarding this particular Prince.

TRUST

Trust is the bedrock of a loving and healthy relationship....
Without it, the relationship will not be viable.

If you do not trust your Prince ... or have lost your trust in
him and are dismal about recapturing it, consider moving on.

Fidelity is only a minute component of trust.... Many people
never stop to realize that trust weaves its way through every
particle of the relationship. The further into the relationship you
proceed, the more extensive the trust list becomes. At the
"Keeper" dating stage, it is safe to assume the unwritten
contract is to trust that he will not cheat on you or intentionally
hurt you, that he will respect you and be tactfully honest. If you
are married, you trust that he will support you, stand by you in
hard times, care for you in sickness, handle the money openly
and honestly, share his feelings, and that you will present a
united front regarding the parenting of your children. These are
only a few aspects in which trust is present. The list is limitless.

**Experiencing each other as Reliable is a notion of trust that
cannot be overemphasized in the context of a
relationship....** In order to sustain a healthy and loving bond,
mutual reliability is a must. Being reliable encompasses
accepting responsibility for *actions* as well as *words*.

FEELINGS

There are four major feelings ... Mad, Sad, Glad, Scared....
The rest are derivatives, combinations, or simultaneous contrary
mixes (ambivalence). (See exercise section.)

**A derivative feeling is one that is rooted in one of the major
four....** For example, "irritated" would be a derivative of MAD;
"ecstatic" would be a derivative of GLAD.

**A combination feeling is a mixture of more than one feeling
at the same time....** For example, "jealous" is a combination of
MAD and SCARED or MAD, SCARED, and SAD.

**An ambivalent feeling is a simultaneous and contradictory
feeling....** For example, you may be simultaneously GLAD,
SAD, and SCARED as you wave good-bye to your firstborn
child who is leaving home to go off for her first year of college.

Hidden feelings ... "Under" the feelings that you are most
aware of, are often other feelings. For example, you may be
mad at your Prince for forgetting your date, but as you explore
deeper inside yourself, you discover that you are also hurt, sad,
scared, shamed, or a combination. Mad was the smoke screen.
The *real* feelings were *hidden* under "mad."

Safe feelings ... The *first* feeling that you experience is usually
the *safe* feeling. In your family of origin certain feelings were
granted more permission to own than others. Those are the *safe*
feelings. Underneath the safer feelings, lie those which you feel
more shame about because they were not "permitted" in your
family. Stereotypically, boys are "allowed" to be mad and girls
are "allowed" to be sad. However, there are MANY exceptions.
Some families promote anger regardless of gender, others

prohibit ALL feelings. A good way to discover what feelings lie underneath your safe ones is to learn your family of origin's "rules" (taught NON verbally through actions and body language) regarding existence, ownership and expression of feelings.

To succeed in a healthy and loving relationship ... you must reach "below your safe feelings " to find the *true* ones. Then you need to SHOW them. Your partner cannot *know* your feelings if you do not express them.

A hallmark of the human condition is that you reside in a state of paradox.... At the *same* moment, and with the *same* amount of vehemence, you may love and hate; desire and not desire; be attracted and repulsed; want to be fused and detached; together and apart; independent and dependent; secure and adventurous; close and far away; joining and competing. This simultaneous co-existence of an infinite variety of opposing forces generates internal chaos as well as relationship turmoil. Recognizing that these conflicting energies dwell in the human psyche allows for greater inner calm and more productive partner negotiation.

Do *not* assume that a derivative, combination,or ambivalent feeling means the same to him as it does to you.... For example, when you say that you are "upset" it may mean that you are sad. When he says that he is "upset" it may mean that he is mad. Upset can mean sad, mad, scared, or a combination of all three feelings. Prod, probe, and paraphrase until you are confident that you understand *exactly* what both you and he are feeling. (See exercise section.)

Do *not* assume ... that his hidden and safe feelings are the same as yours. (Or that because he is male, his safe feeling is anger.)

Feelings are internal reactions to *perceptions*.... This is one reason why "checking out" your perceptions is so important. You want to be sure you are reacting to what you *think* you are reacting to.

Feelings cause your body chemisty to change.... Notice what physical sensations you have when you are feeling mad, sad, glad, and scared. (See exercise section.)

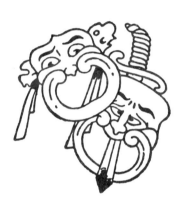

Feelings just *are*.... You have no control over them. You *do* have control over how you *react* to your feelings.

Do not judge your feelings.... Embrace them. You will have better command over your behaviors surrounding those feelings.

As hard as it is to believe ... you *do* have control over your thoughts. You may stop them or change them.

If you are successful at changing your *thoughts* about an issue ... your *feelings* will often change regarding that concern. (See exercise section.)

COMMUNICATION

Communication is the *bridge* that links two people.... In order to maintain a healthy and loving relationship, each of you must know what is transpiring emotionally, physically, and spiritually with the other. The way to transmit this information is by talking and listening.

In order to be a proficient communicator ... you must *know* what you are feeling. You cannot honestly share yourself with another if you do not know your own feelings. (See exercise section.)

There are three skills that you need to learn in order to master the "art" of communication: ... Listen, Talk, Negotiate.

Effective Communication is ... direct, clear, succinct, specific, tactful, respectful, precise, honest.

Effective communication is usually hindered by: poor modeling in the family of origin, faulty messages acquired in the family of origin, low self-esteem, and lack of communication skills..... Most of you reading this guide grew up in households with little or no modeling regarding effective communication. In other words, you did not observe your parents proficiently communicating in healthy and loving ways. You were also given strong messages about feelings and thoughts, which you lived without question. For example, you may have been punished when you expressed anger. The message transmitted was that "anger is *not* OK." When you have been given unhealthy injunctions, that you may not even recognize that you hold, how can you expect to *effectively* share feelings as an adult? Insight is the first step, but insight alone will not do the trick.

To change your "imperfect" communication style ... you must *unlearn* faulty attitudes and behaviors and *learn* new ones. To succeed with this goal, discover what faulty "credos" you are carrying, then "rewire" your brain by getting rid of the "defective" tapes and installing new ones. Improve your self-love so that you will risk exposing your honest feelings and be less vulnerable to "devastation" if your partner is hurtful, judgmental, or rejecting. *Learn* proper communication skills and most importantly, *practice* using your newfound skills and attitudes.

The *way* you say something (choice of words and tone) ... is often much more powerful than *what* you say.

Always speak using "I" statements (as opposed to "you" statements).... "I" statements imply that you are taking responsibility for what you are saying and feeling. "You" statements presume that the other is to blame and immediately put the receiver on the defensive. Compare the different messages you send when you say, "You make me feel incompetent," versus, "I feel incompetent when I am told that I cannot do anything right."

Instead of asking a question ... "Where were you until 1:00 a.m.?" make an "I" statement: "When you hadn't called by 1:00 a.m., I was afraid you had been in an accident." This will put him at ease and you are more likely to get the response you are seeking. If you become accusatory, he will withdraw and/or counterattack.

Beware of methods you may be using to deflect effective communication.... It may be that the reason your man is not talking or responding is because *you* are in some way blocking the process. Pay attention to your body language, words, and tone. Are you creating a safe harbor in which to share?

There is a reason why women are stereotyped as "nags".... (and men as "emotionally unavailable.") Often, the more you nag, the more emotionally closed down he becomes. The more emotionally closed down he becomes, the more you nag. The cycle perpetuates itself. If this issue does not get repaired, the behaviors become more polarized over time ... making it harder and harder to stop what have become automatic reflex behaviors. A successful relationship requires that both genders fix these "accusations." Otherwise you are destined to divorce court or a "life of quiet desperation."

Doing nothing is both a choice and a behavior.... The "nothing" act usually takes you out of the "driver's seat" and puts you on the "passenger" side. In other words, you become less in control of the outcome than if you had made an *active* decision.

A silence may be sacred or toxic.... Know the difference.

Using silence as a combat tool ... very effectively blocks the line of communication. It is a form of "below the belt" fighting as its intent is to render the "opposing party" powerless. The strategy usually works because the recipient feels abandoned.

Do not confuse toxic silence with a "time-out." ... A toxic silence is an unfair fighting technique and a "time-out" is an opportunity for an impasse to be broken by allowing each person a chance to regroup and reflect with the understanding that at a later date, they will return to the challenge ready to resolve it. Usually, the person who has requested the "time-out" is the one to suggest the return date.

Festering anger *will* result in loss of romantic and/or marital bliss ... and may lead to serious physical and/or emotional disease.

Anger does not disappear on its own.... It needs to be directly, respectfully, and appropriately "kicked out."

Never go to bed angry.... What if he dies in his sleep? You will end up with regret *in addition* to your grief.

Many men are not taught to expose their emotions the way women are.... If you are the one who often needs to initiate conversations that involve sharing feelings, settle for it ... as long as he is receptive, fully participates, and takes responsibility once the discussion is in play. Why waste energy being resentful about something you can easily manage? This is one of those situations in which you are "equal, but not the same." It is also true that some women are not taught the skills of recognizing and exposing their feelings. If you are one of these women, get busy learning more about your feelings and how to communicate them.

When there is a doubt about what he means (and vice versa) ... PARAPHRASE! Paraphrasing is defined as repeating in your own words what you understood him to say. He then confirms that you are right, or he will rephrase ... and you will continue reiterating (restating) until he is satisfied that you have understood him. Grasping what he has said does NOT mean that you have to agree. The practice of paraphrasing forces the listener to LISTEN. It also serves as a diffusion of energy when conflicts are involved. "Advanced paraphrasing" involves understanding the *feelings* "behind" the words. (See exercise section.)

Keeping issues "in hiding" ... slowly erodes the relationship.

FIGHTING and DISAGREEMENTS

If you are having a PROBLEM in the relationship ... getting married, having a child, or putting an addition on the house is *not* going to solve it.

When the relationship has existed long enough to discover that there are true differences ... what usually happens is that the couple decides that the way to solve the conflict is to have one "come around" to the other's thinking/feeling. The power struggle begins and the focus of energy is then on the *power struggle* rather than the *issue* that needs resolution! For example: He wants to play first and do chores later. You want to do chores first and play later. He views you as rigid; you view him as irresponsible. The power struggle ensues. You *want* to make him responsible and he *wants* to make you fluid. This is a *waste* of your respective energies. Neither of you will change because of a power struggle. In fact, you will get more locked into your positions! The *issue* is that he wants to play first and you want to do the chores first. The *challenge* is to *negotiate* this difference in such a way that *both* of you are satisfied. The truth is that you each have something important to learn from the other with respect to these opposing positions. Persistent effort in remembering to care, and allowing time to effectively communicate, are paramount in the resolution/negotiation of these differences.

When an argument arises, one of the greatest temptations is to throw the "kitchen sink" into the battle.... The *only* purpose this serves is diversion from the current issue. When you get into a disagreement, focus *only* on that issue. DO NOT BRING UP ANY OTHER PROBLEMS OR RESENTMENTS if you wish to resolve the one at hand.

How you behave (act) will directly affect how he behaves....
If you approach him reasonably, it is more likely that he will respond in kind. If you feel "incapable" of acting or reacting judiciously, take a "time-out" to collect yourself.

If you are the one who cannot match your opponent with clever words in a dispute ... tell him that if he wants you to stay engaged, he must grant you a "time-out" (allowing you to collect your thoughts). You will never win at the "word game." Conversely, if you are the "attorney" and you want your partner to stay tuned in, give him the time and space he needs to collect his thoughts. Under this arrangement, the person who has requested the "time-out" commits to a date, time, and hour in which he/she will share his/her reflections and resume where the impasse left off ready to resolve the challenge.

"Time-out" is *not* synonymous ... with dismissing or "forgetting" the concern. Often when the "storm" has passed and the "waters" appear calm (as a result of the "time-out"), the participants nonverbally "collude" with each other *not* to resurface the issue for fear of another "eruption." This is one of the roots of the demise of a relationship. If the issue is *not* resolved, it *will* rear its ugly head at a later date!

If you reach an impasse ... write him a letter. This will give you an opportunity to express your feelings and him a chance to mull over what you have said.

When the couple is "stuck," it may be sufficient if only one "stretches." ... Just be sure you are not the one who is *always* doing the "stretching." What has usually happened when the couple gets "stuck" is that they have entered into a "power struggle." When one stretches (initiates reaching beyond his/her emotional comfort zone or predictable "role"), it often loosens the rigid stance of the couple, allowing the power struggle to evolve into a negotiation.

If the "stretch" doesn't move you into negotiation ... don't despair. Sometimes all that is needed is TIME for the "wounded parties" to recover from the "power struggle battle."

Do not ignore the "baby elephant" in the middle of the living room.... You both know he is there. The longer you let him stay, the bigger he gets ... allowing for less and less room to maneuver around him. (The "baby elephant" is the problem that is not being addressed.)

Both of you need to have the ability to apologize....
Apologies are a necessary requirement if you want to maintain a healthy and loving relationship. We are continuously making mistakes. If we will not admit our errors and apologize for them, we cannot grow. If we do not grow, the relationship dies.

Always fight fair.... Most of us have failed miserably at this one. However, it is important to continue to strive for this goal. As relationships "age," a history of "below the belt" fighting will cripple them. An example of unfair fighting mentioned in the COMMUNICATION section is the use of silence as a combat tool. Another example would be humiliating him in an area in which he feels extremely vulnerable (his baldness, his inability to maintain an erection ...).

"Sticks and stones will break my bones, but names"...
"WILL hurt me, hurt him, and the relationship, too!" Once you

have said something, it cannot be taken back. Words are never forgotten.

Sometimes a "leap of faith" is necessary, to emerge from the darkness.... You have a challenge. You have the commitment, you have done the "work," and still your progress toward resolution is not obvious. You are both depleted. Take the leap, jump into "the void" of not knowing how it will all turn out, and hang out there together for a while. Don't force the issue. When you are secure that you have done all you can do, "turn it over to the Universe," and trust that she will direct the way.

If despair hits ... view it as the "darkness before the dawn." Many think despair is the "end." On the contrary, it is an opportunity. It is the reflection of the bottom of the pit. From the bottom of the pit, there is nowhere to go but up. It is a "calling" to renew the marriage. It is also a time that generally indicates a need for professional help.

NEGOTIATION

A successful negotiation ... is one in which both parties feel heard by the other. Although neither has gotten what he or she desired, both are encouraged regarding the outcome. Both feel like winners.

An unsuccessful negotiation ... is one in which one is a winner and the other a loser.

A negotiation has a much greater chance for success if ... both parties have the *desire* to have the *relationship* win (as opposed to you or he win).

GRUDGES

The only one being hurt by a grudge is the one holding it.... If you are guilty of grudge holding, unload the resentments as fast as you can. The dump could save your life! If he is a grudge holder, inform him about the physical, emotional, and spiritual risks. If he refuses to "dump" his grudges, consider it a red flag regarding the long-term success of your relationship. (See exercise section.)

Unreleased grudges in a relationship ... jeopardize it!

CARING

Caring involves ... considering your partner from *his* perspective rather than from yours.

Caring involves ... learning the gestures that result in *his* feeling "cared about," rather than assuming that they are the same gestures that elicit *your* experiences of feeling "cared about". For example: *You* may feel "cared about" if he takes five minutes out of his work day to call you, just to say "hi." *He* may feel irritated if you call him in the middle of his work day. *He* may feel "cared about" if you get up to fix breakfast for him. *You* may want to have the house to yourself in the morning and prefer that he *not* get up to fix breakfast for you. The *only* way to discover what each of you consider to be caring gestures is to ask! (See exercise section.)

The "routine" caring acts are often more vital than the extravagant ones.... We all feel cared about when the Prince surprises us with an all-expenses-paid, two-week vacation to the destination of our dreams. It is the ongoing, small, caring acts, like unexpectedly picking up the dry cleaning or bringing home "take-out" on *your* night to cook, that mark the prognosis for a long-term successful relationship.

These caring gestures are the "lubrication" ... that keep the relationship out of danger during the hard times.

INTIMACY

Withholding information erodes intimacy.... When you are intentionally withholding information, you are building a wall around this information to protect it. The problem is that this wall also becomes a barrier between you and your partner. In order to succeed with intimacy, there can be no walls.

Intimacy ... is usually avoided because we are so afraid of pain and suffering.

A major cause of an inability to achieve intimacy is ... lack of self-love. When there is self-love, you know you will "survive" a rejection and therefore you are able to take greater risks in the realm of initiating and sharing intimacy.

Intimacy is not easy to attain ... because in this circumstance, neither of you hold anything back. You are both vulnerable. You each expose parts of yourself that are of a very personal nature. You are fully available to one another, spiritually, emotionally, and physically. For couples fortunate enough to achieve this state, the experience is fleeting, since the human condition is only capable of sustaining this level of exposure for brief periods of time. Frolic during those short-lived moments, and strive to have more!

You will be able to fully revel in those fleeting moments of intimacy ... if you have mastered the skill of not "losing yourself" in the relationship and are not paralyzed by the fear of abandonment and/or engulfment.

You know you are experiencing a moment of intimacy ... when you have no place to hide and you are excited about it!

Striving for intimacy does not mean letting go of all self-protection mechanisms.... It is healthy to have *some* defense mechanisms. If you had none, you would "bruise" too easily. However, most of us wear far too much armor.

It is NOT a foregone conclusion that men and women will remain on separate planets.... It is true that there *are* differences between the genders. It need not be that these variances continue to hold males and females segregated from one another. The path toward integration is discovery of each other's worlds. Compatibility and harmony are more easily attained when understanding and compassion for the other gender are expressed. Gaining this understanding and compassion also enhances self-growth. With polarity, *competition* is born. Discerning the art form of *cooperation* is categorically more gratifying ... physically, emotionally, and spiritually.

MASKS

Masks are worn to play a role on stage ... not to be donned in an intimate relationship.

Masks are created very early in life ... to "be" what we perceive our primary caretakers want us to "be" so that they will love and accept us.

We put on whatever mask we think will work ... in order to be loved and accepted by those we "need" (want) to have love and accept us.

Many of us have had the masks in place for a lifetime.... It may take a while to decipher the true self from the masked role.

Masks must be relinquished ... in order to attain REAL intimacy.

Shedding the masks are liberating ... and scary.... It takes courage to join the world and the relationship as your true self. But, is it not far worse to know that you are "loved" as an impostor?

Give up your masks ... if you want to succeed in a healthy and loving relationship!

EXPECTATIONS AND MYTHS

Someone is NOT better than no one! ... Misery does *not* love company when it comes to being *in* the miserable relationship.

You will be far less miserable alone ... than in a miserable relationship!

Do not deny that the relationship is laden with expectations.... Discover what they are, so that they may be addressed. (See exercise section.)

Unspoken expectations ... *always* exist in a relationship. The marriage package highlights them. Dedicate certain "check-in" times to articulate these "hidden agendas". (See exercise section.)

Exposing hidden expectations ... sometimes prevents them from playing an unconscious and potent role in the marriage.

"He doesn't love me when".... Couples are consistently getting into trouble when they read particular behaviors committed by the other as a direct reproach to themselves. For example, if it is important to me to keep the scotch tape in a certain drawer, I am very likely to interpret his returning it to the *wrong* drawer as, "he doesn't love me." Returning the tape to the wrong drawer does *not* mean "he doesn't love you." What it *does* mean is that he is absent-minded and/or not paying attention and there may be many reasons for that, none of which pertain to you. When these acts occur ... and they will, make an appointment to talk about them rather than attempting to ignore the behaviors. If you ignore the acts, they will accumulate and by the time they are brought up, your feelings will be too intense to have a rational discussion. Sometimes the behaviors *are* intentional. Having the discussion while you are still calm allows for the opportunity to discover the real reason why these acts are happening.

Needing to "decompress" (have time to himself) after a long day at the office ... does *not* mean he does not love you. It means he has not yet successfully "shifted gears" and needs time to do so. If this is a regular occurrence, you may need to negotiate how to successfully "shift gears" together.

One of the biggest mistakes couples make is to abide by the myth which declares that ... "if you loved me, you would know what I want, need, think, and feel, and you would give it to me." ... Love has nothing to do with *knowing* what your partner wants, needs, thinks, and feels.... The only way you will discover these things about each other is by asking and telling. Love also does not guarantee "being given what you want." That craving is a remnant from the past in which you are expecting your partner to parent.

It is commonly believed that "the perfect marriage" is one in which there are no significant differences.... This is a myth! If you think you have no significant conflicts, one person is asleep and/or the other is making major compromises.

Expel the myth of "the perfect marriage is one in which there are no conflicts" ... and strive for a marriage in which you endeavor together to meet your challenges and transitions directly, responsibly, courageously, honestly, patiently, carefully, respectfully, and inexhaustibly!

Some couples have difficulty with "re-entry" when one has been away on a trip.... This is not an automatic indication that there is a problem in the relationship. If you have a concern, do not go underground with it; discuss it.

In relationships there are only perceptions, not realities.... The goal is to meet and understand each other's perceptions.

It takes TWO to dance successfully ... and TWO to flub the step.... Many people believe that *one* person is "causing the problems" in the relationship. This is a myth! If you think *you* are the problem, you are suffering from a different "character flaw" than if you think the "problem" lies with your partner. In either situation, buying into this theory is just another way to keep the relationship stuck.

VALUES

Know your value structures ... but don't be snared by them.

In the Romantic Stage of Love ... the focus is on *similarities*. We see ourselves as compatible because we enjoy the same movies, food, and vacation spots.

In the Romantic Stage of Love ... *differences* are ignored. Political and social class views of the world are not a concern.

As the relationship progresses, these perspectives can become grave points of contention. The more extreme the differences, the more seriously you may want to consider the viability of the relationship, since most every decision made in some way incorporates a political or social class position. (Where you will live, how you will spend your money, how you will raise your children, how each other's family of origin will be integrated into your family system, how elder care will be managed, role expectations, what form your sexual relationship will take, your wishes, hopes, and dreams....) Do NOT minimize the challenge involved in resolution of dissimilar value structures.

BOUNDARIES

The inability to set boundaries for yourself, what you will and will not do, what you will and will not tolerate, ... drastically interferes with your achievement of self-love.

Your unwillingness to set boundaries with him, and everyone else in your life, including your children ... will radically hinder your chances of reaching self-love.

A Boundary in the relationship is ... a limit you set with him, and he sets with you.

The establishment of boundaries is *essential* ... in healthy and loving relationships.

Make sure he is respecting your boundaries ... and you are respecting his.

Imagine a sandbox.... Contained in this sandbox is the person, and *all* that is related to her ... her personal space (the invisible barrier she creates around her body into which no one goes without permission), her physical space (a room in the house, a corner in a room), her body, her spirit, her God, her possessions (including her money), her friends, her time, her thoughts, her feelings, her personal history, her personal interests ... anything and everything pertaining to her SELF and to her LIFE. Every person (including children) on the planet owns a sandbox in which he/she resides, along with all that belongs to him/her. This sandbox and *all* that is embraced within require boundaries that must be negotiated when you enter into a relationship.

Your sandbox is *your* sandbox ... his sandbox is *his* sandbox.... You do *not* belong in each other's sandbox without an invitation. (See exercise section.)

You learned about boundaries in your family of origin.... He learned about boundaries in his family of origin.... As a result, your boundaries may be porous, a closed door may be unthinkable, a private thought nonexistent. Time on your own, or pursing individual interests, may be preposterous. A vacation without him might be inconceivable. On the other hand, his boundaries might be rigid, a closed door might be the norm, his thoughts might always be private. Before he met you, he might have done everything on his own. The collision course is apparent. You each absorbed very different messages in your family of origin, and prior to this relationship, you had no reason to doubt what you learned. The "trick" is to acknowledge that both of your styles are valid. That *negotiation* is required. The "trap" that many fall into is to accuse the other of "wrongdoing," immediately resulting in a defensive posture on the part of the "accused." This "indictment" polarizes, and movement becomes paralyzed. Effective negotiation of boundaries is both one of the most challenging, as well as one of the most rewarding, tasks of the relationship.

What TIME is yours, mine, ours? What SPACE is yours, mine, ours? What MONEY is yours, mine, ours? What DUTIES are yours, mine, ours? What DECISIONS are yours, mine, ours? What POSSESSIONS are yours, mine, ours? What THOUGHTS, FEELINGS, EXPERIENCES and SECRETS are yours, mine, ours? ... These are some of the most obvious boundary issues that all couples need to begin grappling with long before the "final commitment." The boundary list is endless. Effective communication, self-awareness, self-love, and a deep caring for the other are the keys to superior negotiation.

Most couples are either too fused or too disengaged.... When you are too fused you do everything together; you do not know where one leaves off and the other begins. You are "joined at the hip." If you find yourself saying "we" when you really mean "I," you are probably in a fused relationship. When you are too disengaged, you are living together but you each have separate lives. You have no friends or interests in common. You are "two ships passing in the night." If you find yourself thinking in terms of "I," yet you are still half of a "we," you are probably in a disengaged partnership. Both extremes put the relationship in jeopardy. The goal is to find the balance.

In a marriage ... unresolved boundary issues could propel you into a "life of quiet desperation" or divorce.

Which decisions will be made by whom, and whose needs will be most important when ... are matters that need to be seriously addressed before the commitment stage. For example, if both of you have very gratifying jobs and one is asked to relocate, how will you resolve the situation? Likewise, if you decide to have children under the same circumstances of mutually satisfying careers, how will child care be handled?

The healthy resolution of boundaries ... is to find the balance between rigidity and fluidity.

A consequence of having separate interests, friends, and experiences ... is that it enriches the bond. Just be careful not to slip into a "disengaged" relationship. Remember to always strive for the balance between "fused and disengaged."

SEX IN SINGLE LIFE

When you decide that it is time to have sex ... don't waste energy mind reading. Ask him what he likes and tell him (and/or show him) what pleases you. If he is not interested in learning what delights you, this may be a warning of heartaches to come. Consider the viability of the relationship.

Do not confuse lack of sexual education with lack of interest.... Sometimes it is the "hunk" who is least informed when it comes to pleasuring partners. Think about it: he has never had to master the skills, because women date him in spite of his poor lover status. Give him the opportunity to learn, but move on quickly if it becomes clear that he simply is not interested in developing the talent.

It is *not* unromantic to insist that your partner shower before sex ... and he deserves the same from you.

It is NOT his problem if *you* do not know what turns you on.... It is *each* partner's responsibility to arrive at sexual fulfillment with the "help" of the other.

Men were responsible for women's sexual satisfaction in the 50s.... The 60s (women's movement) changed that view; however, many are still living with the 50s mentality which ultimately puts more pressure on both partners.

Learn what turns you on ... and then teach it to your partner.

Sharing a "colorful" sex history with your women friends may be fun.... With your guy ... share slowly and gently. Or, perhaps not at all. Most men do not *really* want to hear the details of your sexual history! If he begins to share his "sexual stories" and you are not interested, ask him to stop.

There are no magic number of dates after which sex is "acceptable" ... (or "unacceptable").... Each situation is different. If you listen to your inner voice you will know when the right time is for you.

If you decide on exclusive sex ... it is imperative that both of you get tested for HIV and other sexually transmitted diseases.

Until you trust him implicitly ... practice Safer Sex! After all, how easy do you think it will be for your partner to tell you he has cheated? Remember ... unprotected sex could cost you your life ... or, at the very least, an unplanned pregnancy.

Intermittent use of birth control devices ... is almost as ineffective as no use of birth control.

If you are old enough to have sex ... you are old enough to do it responsibly.

The use of alcohol may increase sexual desire, impair sexual responsibility (practicing safer sex), and diminish sexual potency.... A male may experience difficulty maintaining his erection and/or achieving orgasm. A female may have difficulty achieving orgasm.

The use of nicotine may decrease sexual potency.... The most frequent complaint regarding the use of this drug is erection difficulty, especially in older males.

The "sex and recreational drugs" issue is more complex.... Some drugs heighten libido, some lessen it; some enhance performance, some diminish it. Most of these drugs have a psychological effect, which can lead to either risky sexual behavior or unwarranted inhibition. These effects may vary depending on the individual, the drug, and the quantity of the drug ingested. Expect that if you are using recreational drugs during sex, those drugs will affect your sex life and the development of your relationship.

Your partner will disclose a major clue regarding his past risky sexual behavior (his practice of unprotected sex) if ... he does *not* insist on wearing a condom with you.

Never engage in sexual practices that make you uncomfortable.... If you do not consent, it is RAPE.

Many men confuse sex and affection.... Since, younger men, especially, tend to get aroused during affectionate exchanges, it is important not to "tease" them, since this will discourage their interest in learning the difference between sex and affection.

"Teasing" is defined as ... "encouraging" sexual arousal by engaging in obvious sexual foreplay, then either "denying" its existence, withdrawing, or refusing to gratify on a regular basis.

Affection is affection and sex is sex ... and it is usually the woman who knows the difference. If you want to have a partner who enjoys affection without sex, teach him the differences and make it fun. Most men will learn to enjoy affection without sex if they know that you are also invested in having sexual contact.

When a woman is *not* interested in a sexual encounter, she will often take the "easy way out" by simply refusing to engage in *any* form of physical contact.... This is because she has had a history of "feeling obligated and sometimes forced" to have sex when she didn't want to, simply because her partner became aroused. Instead of taking the "easy way out," state your desires at the outset giving him the choice. If he concedes to affection without sex, take the risk. You will both benefit from the experience.

Affection without sex can be gratifying.... Invite your partner to explore and enjoy the differences. If he agrees, do not pull away if he becomes physically aroused. He has consented not to pursue sex; his physical arousal is out of his control.

Negotiation rules apply in the bedroom just as in any other room of the house.... If you are always engaged in what *he* desires (particular routines of sex or sex with very little foreplay, etc.) before you consider dumping him, be sure you are making your wishes known. If you are certain that it is not your negotiation skills that are lacking, consider moving on.

Behavior in the bedroom is often a microcosm of the relationship.... If things are not to your satisfaction in the sexual arena, it is usually only a matter of time before the other areas of the relationship will begin to show their cracks.

If you are *only* interested in affection and *never* interested in sex ... consider getting professional help.

Although the most widely held view is that ... "the man is always the one most interested in sex," ... there are many relationships in which this is *not* the case. You are *not* defective if your libido exceeds his.

If the *only* thing that is working well is the sexual relationship ... seek professional help or move on (unless sex is all you are interested in). Although many women express a *desire* to be only interested in sex, most women become emotionally involved and "expect" more once sex has been introduced into the relationship.

CHILDREN

If you want kids ... raising children is the most important job you will ever have.

If you do not have kids of your own ... watch him interact with other people's children. If you have them, how does he blend? How does he take care of his own? It is vital that the Prince pass this "test." If he fails miserably, push on. (Even if you do not intend to have children, how he interacts with kids is usually a good indicator of his "true self.")

How *you* handle the issue of dating with your children ... will affect how receptive they are to new men in their lives. A "constant stream" of prospective stepdads is probably going to be stressful on them. Only introduce the men who are rather serious candidates. Be vigilant about who and how many you allow to "stay over." No matter how clever you deem your strategies regarding overnight guests, you are *not* fooling the older children.

Since management (or lack thereof) of children is one of "the Big Three" predictors of divorce ... if coupling with this man is a possibility, it is critical *from the beginning* to attend to the challenges regarding how the children will be "incorporated" into the relationship. The circumstances will be different depending on whether one or both of you have children, where the children live, how old they are, etc. What is important is that you start talking about and deciding *together* how these issues will be managed.

Take the TIME to establish rules regarding each partner's role vis-a-vis the other's children.... If you do not do this

BEFORE disagreements ensue, you are in for much heartache in the future.

If any of his kids are unruly with you and/or yours with him ... the responsibility for correcting these actions lies with the parent of the difficult children. Insist on certain standards by which they are required to behave. If you do not instill these rules at the beginning, you will not be successful in making them later on.

If he has children who live in his home ... before you get too far into the relationship you had better do your own homework regarding whether you want to raise children. The reality is that once you are in the house you will probably be expected to take on the duties of motherhood.

If you have children living in your home ... has he passed your test of "stepfathering"? If not, at a minimum, do not start living together until the children are out of the home. As stated earlier, how people behave with children is usually a good predictor of their "true self." If he is not conducting himself acceptably with your kids, you may want to consider moving on.

If he is a "weekend Dad" ... how involved is he with his children? Do you like them? Do they like you? Does he insist on a certain standard by which they are required to "treat" you. If there are major problems regarding how his children engage with you and what *he* does about it, do not fool yourself into believing that since they do not live with him it will not be a problem in *your* relationship. Also do not conclude that *you* will be able to fix the problem. (The difficulty lies between him and his children.) Insist on addressing this challenge before you become more involved. If he refuses to acknowledge or denies the importance of this "concern," you will save yourself much undue suffering if you get out now.

It is essential that parents be in agreement with one another regarding the guidance of their children.... You may share differences of opinions in front of them, as long as you demonstrate healthy ways to express these opposing views and *ultimately* support each other with a united decision. It is important for the children to know that they will *not* be successful at dividing you.

It is *never* acceptable to fight in front of the kids.... Modeling disagreements that are handled maturely is permissible. Kids know that differences exist. Show them how to negotiate constructively. If you are not confident that you can "pull it off," don't take the chance. It is far better to resolve your clash in private, than to risk deteriorating from a *discussion* to *combat* in their presence.

It is the nature of children to love those who care for them.... In a blended marriage situation, the children are sometimes "instructed" by the natural parent not to love the stepparent. There is *nothing* to gain by giving them this message. Allow children to maintain their nature of loving those who care for them. Loving a stepparent will *not* take away their love for the natural parent.

Remember that children learn what they observe.... Teach them how to have a healthy and loving relationship by being in one.

POWER AND CONTROL

Power (inner strength) and Control are NOT interchangeable concepts.... The underlying feeling driving power is *joy*. The underlying feeling driving control is *fear*.

The goal is to gain Power (inner strength) and to let go of Control.... Remember that control is an illusion. You *actually* have no control over any other person, place, or situation.

Within a controlling person ... lies a fearful person.

An "openly" controlling person ... may not *know* he/she is ruled by fear.

A "subversive" controller ... is "subterranean" and usually knows he/she is fearful. A "subversive" controller usually perceives herself as having little or no inner strength.

Both control "tactics" are destructive.... They undermine relationships and rob self-love.

Control is a *dysfunctional* strategy ... used to defend against what we fear most, the possibility of being engulfed and/or abandoned. Inner strength guards against the anxiety associated with abandonment and engulfment. An inwardly powerful person can hold boundaries to keep from being "swallowed up," and feel "whole" enough to not be so concerned about being deserted.

When there is power (inner strength) ... there is no need to control, openly or subversively. One may give and receive artlessly. Needs, wishes, and desires may be expressed directly. Decisions may be made consciously.

Take care of yourself first.... Do "damage control" second. Taking care of yourself first sometimes disrupts your partner's needs. "Damage control" means that you are attending to and "working through" the effects on the relationship (and him), when you take care of yourself first.

OUT OF YOUR CONTROL

The Serenity Prayer ... *"God grant me the serenity to accept the things I cannot change, courage to change the things I can, and the wisdom to know the difference."* Reinhold Niebuhr

Read the "Serenity Prayer" again and again.... At times that may be all you can do when you feel mad (or powerless), that you cannot control, change, or "improve" (in your opinion) a person, place, or situation.

A leopard will not change his spots ... but *he* can *choose* to change his *behavior*.

You CANNOT change him! ... no matter how motivated you are to do so.

You cannot be his savior ... or his mother.... He may insinuate that he wants to be saved and/or to be mothered. But, he will resent you if you "take the bait." Make him aware of his behavior.

Changing a playboy is not within *your* realm of capability.... Remember the leopard's spots? Even if he appears differently, he has been a player until you met him, and he most likely will not change now. If you really want to give him a chance, and you have the time ... listen to your intuition step by step. If he IS converting, you will feel an inner sense of calm and joy. If he is NOT, you will feel "ill at ease." Your body will tell you. Listen to her!

All of his Potential and $1.25 is the cost of a cup of coffee.... You may believe you have the power to mold some men into sensitive, intuitive, wealthy, romantic, attentive beings.... When you meet one of these "potentials," you are even more disappointed when he does not accomplish *your* goal. Potential is a TEASE. It means *absolutely nothing* if he does not actualize it.

As soon as you recognize that you are in love with his potential ... get out and let him know why you are leaving. If you wish, make a date with him in the future to see whether he has begun to fulfill his potential, but do not be too optimistic.

PERSONAL GROWTH

"No pain, no gain"... is usually true. Suffering *does* promote personal growth.

Most people will go to extreme measures to avoid healthy suffering ... by arming themselves with dysfunctional behaviors that are far more agonizing. These maladaptive behaviors are learned in our families of origin. Recovery comes from gaining insight with regard to those dysfunctional behaviors and then *changing* them. Change takes time and requires patience, practice, and perseverance. Acquiring the insight without putting it into action will *not* change the dysfunctional behavior.

To know that you *both* hold the inner strength to walk away and thrive if the relationship is no longer viable ... paradoxically results in a considerably higher probability that the relationship will succeed.

YOUR PARTNER'S PERSONAL GROWTH

It is important to determine early on whether *his investment* in personal and relationship growth is compatible with yours.... Since relationships are complicated and require much attention, it is vital that you *each* be motivated to invest about the same amount of time and energy. A commitment involves hard work and the willingness to negotiate differences. Consider that you bought a business together. It is quite obvious that the more work you both put into it, the more likely it will succeed. It is also quite obvious that if only one of you is working in the business, considerable tension will result. The same outcome is guaranteed in your relationship. If your partner is *not* doing his fair share, get out, and devote your time and energy to someone who will.

When the desire for personal growth does *not* come from *within*, the relationship is usually on a dead end course.... You are wasting your valuable time and energy if he is *only* interested in "working on the relationship" because he wants you, rather than because he is *personally* interested in furthering his *own* development.

Do you want him or do you want personal growth? ... You may have to choose. It is very difficult to maintain a relationship if only one of you is growing. If you are the one evolving, you will become bored, sad, scared, angry, or all of the above when your partner refuses to blossom with you. You will either have to stop growing, *or* deal with your feelings associated with his unwillingness to develop. Dealing with those feelings may result in deciding that you have no choice but to leave him, because prior "character flaws" and "bothersome behaviors" now become "intolerable." Although it will hurt to conclude that you need to end the relationship, your insides will nag you "to go" until you finally concede. Although you may be scared to be on your own, your growth will have taught you that you *will* survive. If *he* is the one who is blooming, get going with your own growth spurt if you do not want to be left in the dust!

The fact is, that many gorgeous, exceedingly bright, wealthy, highly educated women will put up with unacceptable behavior from their men.... This results in a "laziness" on the part of some men regarding personal growth. This is not so much a statement about the men as it is about the women who will put up with them. It is the nature of most human beings (men and women alike) to take the "easier road" when presented with a choice. Since there are so many "good" women to choose from, if the woman he is currently involved with becomes "demanding, challenging, or expectant," a number of men, who have not yet invested themselves in the relationship, will simply take the "easy road" and move on to *their* next candidate, rather than the "harder road" of "working through" whatever needs to be addressed.

If *all* women insisted on "good men" ... the men would no longer have the *option* to move on to *their* next prospect.

If *all* women insisted on "good men" ... the men would be "forced" to take "the harder road" which would aid them in *their own* healing and personal growth.

Most men who act like jerks ... do it because women let them!

"YOU CAN CATCH MORE BEES WITH HONEY"

Pay as much attention to what is working well in the relationship ... as you devote to the problem areas. A surprising fact is that it is often more difficult to praise than to criticize.

If you do not SHOW (through words and actions) your loving feelings toward your partner ... you may put the relationship in jeopardy.

Not only is it a waste of your valuable time to "wish" that he be different than he is ... you may be missing who he *really* is.

A relationship in which there is constant criticism eventually dies.... Even if the one being criticized does not physically leave the relationship, he/she will eventually close down and no longer be "in" the relationship.

Positive reinforcement promises more long lasting success than punishment ... when it comes to behavior and attitude changes.

A heartening thing about relationships ... is that they offer *continuous* opportunities for growth and learning. If you miss the chance for a life lesson today, there are always others presented tomorrow! (Or the same one presented in a different cloak.)

Relationships are never completed.... Just when you think you have arrived at a great "resting place," you realize that there is another trail inviting you to even "greener pastures."

At each juncture, you have the option to stop or move forward. The exciting thing about exploring new horizons is that at the "end" of each path walked, greater beauty is promised in the new beginning.

THE DECISION:

Is He a "Keeper" or Is He a "Throwaway"?

The decision phase ... is the period in which you are reviewing and examining the "data" that you have collected over the "keeper" dating period. This is a potentially life-changing time. Remember your gut KNOWS better than ANY guidebook.

ASSESSMENT

The "Rules of the Relationship" are set in concrete by the time you arrive at the commitment stage.... Many believe that dating is the time to discover each other and the commitment phase is when the "rules of the relationship" are established.... This is a myth! The norms that you will live by for the *duration* of the relationship are being formed from the minute you meet. For example, if you compromise a bottom line on the first date ... you are doomed to continue compromising. Need the examples continue?

It is *much* more difficult to salvage a relationship that is already in trouble ... than it is to practice from the beginning establishing the rules and priorities necessary to create a loving and healthy relationship.

Is he Reliable, Responsible, Respectful, Courageous, Kind, Considerate, Patient, Persevering, Caring? ... Does he have the capacity and desire to **commit**? Is he **honest**? Does he appear **forgiving**? Do you **trust** him? Does he **share** his thoughts and feelings with you, and **listen** to yours? Is there **chemistry**? Are you **compatible**? Judge for yourself how many of these questions need to be answered in the "affirmative," in order to qualify him as a keeper. If the only "yes" you checked was "chemistry" ... you may want to consider moving on!

It is ultimately much more gratifying to pick someone who is Self-Aware and willing to do the WORK necessary to sustain a loving and healthy relationship ... than it is to select a famous rich stud.

All the data needed to determine the "status" of your man is in, very soon after you meet.... There is no timetable, however, that may be applied to conclude EXACTLY when "The Decision" need be made.... This is because creating a formula would rob the relationship of it's *own* UNIQUENESS and particular rhythm.

The simple fact is that most women spend FAR too long staying in a "throwaway" situation.... Her gut has known and spoken a long time ago. She chooses NOT to attend to this wisdom because she doesn't like "the decision" her gut has made. She hopes that by hanging in longer ... her gut will see that there has been an error. There was no error! She is your BEST friend! Heed her warnings.... Get OUT , GRIEVE, and move on.

Before you get too far into the relationship, determine whether or not he is AVAILABLE!... The signs are evident at the beginning if you are looking for them. He may be in regular contact with his ex-wife, or he may be "good friends" with his ex-girlfriend. Do not conclude that because the former girlfriend or spouse is deceased, he is no longer tied to her.

Do not be "taken in" by a married man ... who guarantees you that he will get a divorce. Even if he is separated from his wife, the bottom line is that he is UNAVAILABLE.

Regardless of his reasons, become suspicious regarding his availability ... if he doesn't give you his home and work phone number or if he rules that *he* will be the one to make contact with you.

If your pattern is to become involved with "unavailable men" ... you may want to explore your own fears regarding commitment and intimacy.

Do not confuse "emotionally *unexpressive*" with "emotionally *unavailable*".... Many men do a poor job of revealing their emotions. This is *not* the same as being attached to someone else, making it virtually impossible to be *available* to you.

If he tells you early in the relationship that he does not see the two of you together over the long haul ... heed his words. He is probably telling you the truth! Do not conclude that you will change his mind.

Most women are quite well-versed in self-sabotage.... They will throw every rule learned about "self protection in the dating world" out the window when the hormones kick in.

Another form of self-sabotage performed ... is having a generally negative mind set. If you discover you are one of these women, work at dumping it. The release of negative attitudes will not only improve your dating situation, it will change your life!

Turbulence is part of the ride ... at least through the "keeper" dating phase and periodically for the rest of your life. Appreciate that it exists and learn to go with it, rather than resist it! If you master the skill, it will save you an inordinate amount of energy and stress.

There are many reasons why women stay "in" well after it is clear that we need to get "out." ... Take the time to examine WHY you are staying "in." Is it because you are hoping *he* will change, hoping *you* will change him, living by the "rule" that something is better than nothing, afraid of the unknown? Often we stay in a familiar situation because it is easier than risking the unforeseeable consequences of the New. Take the risk! You will have some rocky roads, but you will come to be proud of yourself for having had the *courage* to get out of a bad situation.

The longer you stay IN a bad situation ... the harder it is to get **OUT**.

It may be easier to point out his faults ... than to confront yourself regarding why you continue to stay with him.

Toads can be exciting, charming, and very hard to resist ... but they are still Toads.

Do you prefer *acute* or *chronic* pain? ... If you choose to leave a *bad* situation, the pain will be *acute*, but in time it will end. Staying in a *bad* relationship promises *chronic* pain until you either get out or detach from the situation or person. (Certain fellowship programs such as Al-Anon teach "detachment with love.")

A very important question to ask yourself when you begin to assess the prospect is: "Would I want my best friend or sister dating this guy?"... If the answer is NO, make him history.

Watch him carefully.... How is he behaving with the waitress, his friends, your friends, his children, your children, his dog, your cat, your brother, his mother? How your "Prince" behaves in situations in which he does not know he is being evaluated is crucial in deciding whether this guy is for you. How he acts with the waitress reveals his attitude toward someone "serving" him. Do you notice a difference between how he is with "his people" (his friends, his family) and "your people" (your friends, your family)? The manner in which he treats children and animals lends a "bird's-eye" view regarding his compassion and goodness of heart. Last, but certainly not least, is his treatment of his mother. How he is with her will divulge hints regarding how you will be treated when "the heat" dies down.

If this man is not at least curious about your passionate interests ... move on.

Be careful not to confuse money with love.... Just because he is "spending" money on you does NOT mean that he cares. Notice whether he is "spending" time, energy, and effort on you.

During the "heat" stage of the relationship in which you are both driven primarily by hormones ... it is difficult to "work" on issues that have arisen between you. Once that stage wanes (and it always does), you have three choices: to part, to hurt, or to heal. Unfortunately, many couples opt for parting or hurting (themselves and each other). Those are the easier selections. Healing the self and the other requires an intense desire and willingness to grow and change, as well as the courage to endure the challenging periods during that process.

When the hormones are raging, it is easy to become deluded.... This is the time to ask your roommate, or even your mother, whether he is the Prince. During this phase of the relationship, they can be much more objective.

If you KNOW that your lifelong plans (goals, hopes and dreams), are *in*compatible with his, *but* are hopeful that *after* the marriage you will be able to "change him and/or his mind" ... odds are that you won't! So cut your losses and save yourself a lot of heartache.

Am I aware that "keeping" him means I am also "keeping" his family? ... Don't delude yourself into believing that if his family does not live in your state that you will not have to deal with them. Marry him, and you are marrying the whole family.

Sometimes it *really* is hard to determine whether you have a keeper.... He may have many of the qualities that you are looking for. You may be having great fun with him. Yet, something doesn't "feel" right. Are you afraid to give in to love, or is there a problem? These cases are tricky. There are two things that you may do to help clarify the dilemma: 1) give the relationship more time, and 2) give your inner voice more opportunity to "speak," by quietly listening and journaling. Do not ignore the internal tugs that refuse to rest. If this is a man you would consider marrying yet you continue to remain unsettled, seek professional help.

Missing your singlehood era does not necessarily mean that you are in a bad relationship.... Every new circumstance evokes loss of the "old." In every loss there is grief and in every grief reaction there is anger, fear and sadness. Just be sure that these feelings are not a "cover" for something you are denying that is amiss in the relationship.

WARNING BELLS!

If you have been "keeper" dating for more than three months ... and are not exclusive, have not met any of his friends or family members, have not heard anything about what his feelings are toward you, have not spoken about the future, and are being excluded from a lot of his free time, you may want to point out what you are observing; however, "actions generally do speak louder than words."

If you are "keeper" dating and he is calling you *less* ... it is time to either change your intention in this relationship or move on.

If you are looking for "mutuality and equality" in the relationship ... do not expect that he will pay for every event you attend together. Offer to treat him from time to time. Take equal initiative in deciding what you will do and where you will go. If he is *not* amenable, consider moving on. His "desire" to be in charge is most likely an indication of his attitude regarding the "status" of women and/or his "need" to be in control.

The natural state of a relationship is to vacillate between pursuing and being pursued.... If you are doing all the pursuing and the relationship has just started ... let him go. It is not worth the future headaches and heartaches to keep hanging on. If you have been "an item" for a while, ask him if he has any insight about why you are doing all the chasing. If his answer is unsatisfactory, move on to your next prospect. If he is doing all the pursuing, heed the warning and question yourself regarding why this is. It may be time to take an inventory of the status of the relationship.

If you take an emotional risk and he makes no move to meet you with one in return ... pay attention! Either he is not versed at expressing emotions, but *wants* to learn, or this is a sign of events to come. When you muster up the courage to show your own vulnerability, that act is an invitation for him to show you his. If he consistently will not share his tender spots when you share yours, consider the viability of the relationship.

Letting the Prince control your life is NOT going to lead you to "happily ever after." ... What you have allowed yourself to become is a *victim*. Although victims bear no

responsibility, they also have no freedom.... The choice is yours!

Women are sitting ducks when it comes to "losing themselves" in romantic relationships.... They are ready to "give it all up," including themselves, for the man they love. He is unlikely to "give it all up" for you.... Webster's definition of "to lose" is: to perish, to dissolve, to *destroy*. You were not put on this planet to be *destroyed* by a relationship.

If you are feeling pressure to give up things you want to do, or are frequently the one who "gives in"... and have expressed your concerns, yet continue to have the same experiences, you know what to do.

If he is not ready to go the extra mile in the beginning he won't do it later on.... A major heartache can be saved if you listen to your intuition at the onset. Many women are "experts" at condoning unacceptable behaviors, convincing, understanding, helping, and rescuing. Many women will do just about anything to "hang on." ... Well, don't! ... Grieve, then move on to your next selection.

Just because your prospective Prince is no longer "seeing" his ex ... it does NOT mean he is "finished" with her. One of the often missed signs that business is still unfinished is a connection through anger. Feeling, thinking about, and expressing anger takes a lot of energy. A relationship that is over does not require energy.

Beware if the Prince does his ex's chores, mows her lawn, and/or talks about her a lot.... Regardless of how convincingly and negatively he paints the picture, the fact is ... he is still connected.

Being physically separated from a former partner is *not* the same as being emotionally finished.... Know the difference.

The opposite of love is NOT hate.... It is indifference. Hatred has a certain passion about it. Indifference does not hold passion. A relationship that is "done" no longer contains passion or energy.

If he is lying at the beginning about "little" things ... he will lie about "bigger" things later.

Most of us have been in a relationship in which he "sees the light" and promises to change AFTER the breakup, in order to get you back.... Unless he has changed certain *behaviors* that do not pertain to you, such as joining a 12-step program, entering psychotherapy, and/or exploring his spiritual development ... most likely nothing will be different once the "newness" of your return has "worn off." If you *do* decide to give it another chance, it would be advisable to do it "under supervision" (with a marriage counselor).

If you are involved in a "rebound" or a "transitional relationship" ... the chances are, the relationship won't make it.

BEWARE if you are putting more into the relationship ... than you are getting out of it. Most likely time will not change this dynamic.

OBSESSION and ADDICTION: WARNING BELLS DESERVING SEPARATE MENTION

Having someone obsessed with you is NOT a compliment.... At the very least, it is painful ... at the most ... lethal. Obsession is NOT a sign of love. Rather, it is a warning of danger. Obsession and possession go hand in hand. Notice and beware when he calls you at all hours of the day and night, ignores your limit settings, wants to know your every move, who you talk to, where, when, and why.... It may seem harmless when he shows up at your door without an invitation. In the initial stage of the relationship, it may even be thrilling to have such an "attentive" man, but heed the warnings.... These behaviors are red flags. If you detect any signs of obsession ... RUN!

Extreme sexual jealousy could be a precursor to an "obsessional love." ... If he appears "obsessed" with wanting to know lurid sexual details about your previous encounters, suspects you are sexually interested in other men, or accuses you of flirting with them ... beware.

If you say, "NO!" and your statement is ignored ... this is a warning bell. The less dangerous explanation for dismissing your words, is that he does not know how to listen or that he grew up with no instruction regarding boundaries. The more alarming interpretation is that he is on his way to engulfing, abusing, and/or making you a target of obsession. Evaluate the relationship to decide which it is. Do *not* disregard (or ignore) this signal!

Being addicted to *him* may be hazardous to *your* health.... The stress involved in participating in an addictive relationship at the very least destroys self-love. If the addiction continues, the body begins to weaken and becomes vulnerable to serious illness.

The hallmarks of a relationship addiction are:

- A preoccupation with that person to the exclusion of everyone and everything else, often interfering with or even destroying your ability to effectively manage the other areas of your life, such as taking care of yourself, (see "Healthy Routines," Getting Prepared section), your work, your friends, and your family.
- A compulsion to be in the relationship *at any cost*.
- Panic at the thought of not having him in your life, even when you *know* the relationship is bad.

- The experience of feeling controlled (your actions, your thoughts, and your feelings) by the relationship.
- Urges and impulses so strong that you act on them in spite of potentially embarrassing and/or dangerous consequences.

Being addicted to a person ... replicates many of the same feelings, thoughts, and behaviors as being addicted to a substance.

You may be addicted to him ... if you are doing things that you are embarrassed to tell others about, such as putting up with abusive behavior or driving past his house at midnight to see whether he has company.

If you are engaging in behaviors that he requests of you ... that compromise your integrity, and/or make you feel uncomfortable, the likelihood of addiction needs to be considered.

It is not unusual in a *long-standing* addictive relationship to have the physical "rush" that exists in the *beginning* of a romantic liaison persist.... The "rush" itself becomes the addictive substance, making it almost impossible to exercise the willpower to walk away.

Many addictive relationships exist in which there are *no* physical or emotional highs ... yet the experience is still one of powerlessness regarding the ability to leave it.

It is possible to be addicted to a person you despise or fear.... If you fear or despise him and are identifying with any of the nuggets listed in this section, consider addiction as a possibility.

It is easy to confuse the budding love stage of a relationship with addiction ... since many of the thoughts, feelings, and behaviors are the same. You feel ecstatic, you are strongly attracted to him, you think about him all the time, you cannot imagine your life without him, you want to spend every moment with him, you miss him when you are away from him, you can't wait to see him again, and you cannot get enough of him. The difference is that in the early love stage, you are not being *controlled* by those experiences at the risk of demolishing the other areas of your life. You also are not doing things that embarrass you or put you in harm's way, nor are you engaging in behaviors that compromise your integrity and/or make you feel uncomfortable.

The clues regarding addiction and obsession are present right from the beginning, if we PAY ATTENTION.... The problem is that we do not *want* to notice the warning signs because the sensations of pleasure are so intoxicating.

You can avoid preoccupation with the relationship by having *self love* and a LIFE outside of it! ... Rely on hobbies, friends, and work.

If you have a pattern of becoming addicted to the men you get involved with ... you are probably lacking in self-love and/or replicating an old *unhealed* emotional wound. It is generally a good idea to seek professional help when addiction is a pattern since these types of relationships can be so devastating and dangerous.

If you conclude that you *are* addicted to him ... SLOW DOWN! Re-establish boundaries with yourself and with him. Spend less time with him. Re-involve yourself with the friends and activities that took up your free time prior to this "new love."

A Preoccupation with the relationship is a warning sign that you are "losing yourself." ... If you are unsuccessful at lessening the grip, get professional help!

MARRIAGE CRITERIA

Criteria to evaluate whether he is a marital prospect: ... Ask your friends, your parents, your children for their assessment. Do you have mutual life goals? Do you share similar values? Do you share a similar life philosophy? Are you having fun in the relationship? What are his friends like? Can you live with his chosen career path? Does he make enough money? Is his housekeeping style compatible with yours? Can you get along with his family members? How does he interact with all (male, female, black, white, yellow, red, rich, poor, educated, uneducated) people? How does he behave with animals? Are you stimulated by him? Are you intellectually suited? Are you spiritually in sync? Could you see yourself growing old with him? Would you be willing to take care of him in sickness? Would you allow him to take care of you in sickness? Do you laugh with him? Do you play with him? Do you like him? (It is not enough just to love him.) Can you see him as the father and/or stepfather of your children? Is he committed to personal growth? Is he emotionally open? Does he have *integrity* and *a good heart?* Is he responsible, reliable, courageous, considerate, patient, caring, and forgiving? Is he tactfully honest? Can he be both gentle and firm? Do you trust him? Do you respect him? Does he trust and respect you? Are you sexually attracted to him? Is he sexually attracted to you? Is he affectionate? Does he share his feelings, thoughts, wishes, and dreams with you? Have his behaviors demonstrated that he is committed to WORKING on the relationship? The list is endless ... so *you* have to set your own priorities to make the determination (since he cannot possibly be *all* of the above). (See exercise section.)

PREMARITAL ISSUES TO DISCUSS WITH YOUR PARTNER

Before "tying the knot" ... be sure that you are in agreement regarding whether or not you want children, and if so how many. If he tells you before the marriage that he does *not* want kids, DO NOT count on changing his mind after you are married. Most likely you will be *un*successful! If he *wants* children and you don't, this will be a source of pain in the years to come. The question of whether or not to have kids *needs* to be resolved *before* the marriage. This is an issue in which you cannot come to a compromise. If one wants children and the other does not, one of you will have to "lose," and resentment *will* build. Whether or not to have children is a situation in which if you do *not* agree, the viability of the relationship needs to be considered.

Before the marriage, discuss your views regarding parenting.... How much involvement will each of you have in raising the children? Will they attend private schools? How will you discipline them? How will you handle child care? Will you both work?

Do not omit discussions on ... how aging parents will be cared for.

How finances will be structured and who will manage the money ... needs to be addressed before the marriage. Will either of you arrange for a "prenuptial" agreement?

What role will religion have in your relationship? ... Like it or not, your Sunday School training has had its effect. If there are children involved, what guidance will you give them regarding religious teachings?

What role will spirituality have in your relationship? ... Spirituality and religion are not one and the same, you can have one without the other, neither, or both!

Do you want pets? ... How many, what kind, and who will care for them? Will you have "pet rules," such as large dogs need to attend obedience training?

If you will be entering into a "blended" marriage ... how your respective children will be merged into this marriage needs to be addressed. One of the most frequent causes of second marriage breakups is unresolved integration of children from previous relationships into the new one.

Are you prepared ... not only to be dealing with his family members, but with all of his *internalized* family "tapes" as well? (Many of which *he* may not even be aware of.)

Will you spend the holidays with your extended families? ... If so, how will you negotiate with whom you will spend them?

You may like the color of his skin, but his family may not like the color of yours.... Your challenges are not over just because you and your guy are not concerned about the fact that each of you has a different skin color. His family may be prejudiced and it is you and your children (from a previous marriage and those from this one) who will pay. The same could be true about your family.

Do not minimize other biases (religious preference, social class, level of education, divorced status, etc.), that his family has against you, or your family has toward him.... How you each deal with your respective families right from the beginning, (limit setting) will influence how they will interact with you later on.

Even if you think you have your own family "under control" regarding this marriage ... you don't! Your family can be just as problematic as his. And you, too, have carried all your family baggage into this relationship.

It is not so much that all these issues need resolution *before* the marriage (except whether or not you will have children), ... as it is that you are talking and making yourselves aware of concerns that need attention.

COMMITMENT
AND
MARRIAGE

You have successfully stepped out of the roller coaster ...
and decided to make a commitment with the intention of
marriage. Marriage is merely a continuation of the commitment
phase. There are some situations in which marriage does not
follow commitment such as gays living in states where legal
marriage is not an option, however, in most instances a
commitment is the dress rehearsal preceding opening night.

Staying married today ... is a greater challenge than in
generations past. When people were dead by 30, couples didn't
have to negotiate as many *individual* life transitions *together* as
they face today, where we are living well into our 90s. Sharing
a life with someone while *each* of you go through the
developmental and situational transitions of 60 years can be
quite a challenge.

THE "C" WORD (Commitment)

The paradox of commitment: ... "I will *not* commit to this
relationship until I KNOW it is going to succeed. However, the
only way I am going to know whether this relationship will
flourish is *if* I commit to it." Commitment means that I agree to
"hang in there" through the "hard times" WITHOUT
threatening to leave or retaliate. The reason for this contract is
that, in order to achieve intimacy and resolve conflicts, each
partner needs to be free to be his or her TRUE SELF without
the "threat" of chastisement or abandonment. Making this
"bargain" promotes vulnerability (a critical "intimacy recipe"
ingredient) and dramatically increases investment (motivation)
in problem solution.

The commitment stage ... allows time for correction of challenges or parting of the ways.

In most circumstances a commitment without the marriage (in which marriage is possible) ... robs the relationship of its *full* potential.

There may be some instances in which a couple who may legally marry chooses not to.... If you are in this situation, be sure that your reasons are legitimate and not simply a "rationalization" to avoid commitment.

If your relationship is one in which a legal marriage will not take place ... make a "public declaration" of your commitment. Invite friends and relatives to a celebration in which they witness an exchange of vows and rings.

A commitment means that you agree to take life's journey together ... responsibly, respectfully, and courageously.

A commitment to the relationship does *not* mean that ... you tolerate abuse in *any* form.

A commitment to the relationship does *not* mean that ... you compromise your integrity in *any* way.

A commitment is a PROCESS, not a static state.... The only sure thing about the *process* is that it is changing.

Having the motivation to make a marriage successful cannot be overemphasized.... Relationships are very hard work and there will be times when you will want to "throw in the towel." This is when you need to remember how dedicated and committed you are to achieving and maintaining a loving and healthy marriage.

CHANGE

Relationships change whether we want them to or not ...
because we cannot avoid mutations of external circumstances,
nor can we control wishes, hopes, dreams, growth spurts, and
experiences of our partner (or ourself).

**If you perceive that your relationship hasn't changed since
you met ...** you are either in denial and/or the relationship is
stuck.

If he complains that you have changed ... encourage him to
share his feelings about that. Most likely, he is scared. He may
"accuse" you of not being the person he married. What will be
on the surface is his anger. Usually, what he is really saying is
that he is fearful regarding the stability of the relationship.

You are not the same person at 55 that you were at 25....
Many of your wishes, hopes, dreams, desires, and needs have
changed. At 55, you have lots of life experience; consequently,
your view of the world is markedly different than it was at 25. If
you married at 25 and are still married to the same man, you
have been together for 30 years! Neither of you is the person
who said "I do." Expect and *be grateful* that you have both
changed, yet know that it has *not* been easy to walk beside each
other through crises, growth spurts, and individual life
experiences. Look forward to many more years in which you
will each *continue* to evolve into different people, becoming at
75 someone other than who you are at 55.

Resistance to change ... is normal!

We resist change because ... we fear uncharted territory.

Most of us would rather stay in *familiar* **misery ...** than risk venturing into *unknown* bliss.

You cannot change your relationship ... until you have changed yourself!

When one partner changes there is a "ripple effect" in the relationship.... The shift of *one* partner can either be a threat or a grand opportunity for continued growth in the marriage. Make it a metamorphosis and prepare for a bumpy period while these new attitudes and behaviors are being integrated.

Meaningful Change takes time ... so be patient. Expect two steps forward, one step back. You will know that change has occurred when it endures under stress!

If you are miserable now, it will *not* **spontaneously get better later on....** Fix the problem NOW, or get out! The road you are on if you stay together over the years will bring you a "life of quiet desperation." Eventually you will be too old to leave one another. Most people contract some form of illness in advanced age prior to death. This means that one of you will be caring for the other in sickness. Imagine what it will be like to care *for* or *be* cared for if the relationship is filled with disdain and/or bitterness.

INSTITUTION OF MARRIAGE

The institution of marriage provides a playing field ... in which each partner works on "self-actualization" as well as encouraging the *other* to blossom into his/her fullest spiritual potential. The challenge is to succeed at staying true to yourself while at the same time assisting the other to stretch. This may mean personal suffering when either partner discovers something on his/her path that threatens the stability of the relationship. An example of personal suffering regarding "self-actualization" would be knowing you need to leave the marriage in order to flourish and relegating the children to an upbringing with a "weekend dad" as a result. An example of personal suffering regarding "actualization of the other" would be knowing he needs to leave and loving him enough to *encourage* him to do so, when you so want him to stay. When the institution is viewed as self-serving, the prognosis for a healthy and loving relationship is dismal.

Striving to maintain the balance between nurturing *self*-growth and encouraging growth of the *other* ... is a challenging, *lifelong* process.

The "tests" will present themselves when ... your partner nudges you to stray from your path for his benefit, or when the view of his road threatens you. Passing the tests require that you stay true to yourself while at the same time attending to his needs. An honest discussion in which you each share your fears and desires is the way to sound negotiation. Ignoring the "tests" will *not* make them go away.

Since many men are taught early in life to be self-sufficient (which can turn into self-absorption) ... and many women are taught early in life to be self-sacrificing, it is easy to fall into a dangerous pattern of allowing the husband's desires and needs to be more visible. This results in an imbalance regarding the purpose of the marriage (which is to foster one's *own* and *other's* spiritual growth). One way to monitor this potential pitfall is to notice whether your husband is encouraging *you* to blossom. If not, you have probably fallen into this "trap." To maintain a healthy and loving relationship, this imbalance needs to be fixed. Restoring or creating the equilibrium may take work and patience if your husband has adapted well to your "self-sacrifice" mode.

Self-Absorption (self-centeredness) and Self-Love are NOT the same.... If you are *self-centered*, you are preoccupied exclusively with your *own* wishes, desires, pleasures, and needs, with little or no regard for those of another. If you have *self-love*, your own needs are paramount; however, you are also *highly* invested in the other's wishes, desires, pleasures, and needs.

As a self-centered person ... you will be unable to succeed in a healthy and loving relationship because you are not willing (or able) to experience empathy for your partner, nor willing (or able) to genuinely consider *his* desires, interests, or needs. The extreme of self-absorption is narcissism. (See "Love and Self-Love," Getting Prepared section.)

As a person with self-love ... your chances for success in a healthy and loving relationship are markedly improved. This is because you are *as* dedicated to your partner's well-being as you are to your own. And, because you come to the relationship believing that you are lovable and good enough. When you view yourself as lovable and good enough, you *expect* the world to see you as worthy. As a result, you bring self-confidence (not arrogance) to the relationship. This self-confidence, permits greater presence (attention) in the relationship because you are not wondering what he is thinking (does he like me? will I be ridiculed? will I be hurt?...) while you are interacting. When you are confident, you are capable of setting boundaries thus lessening your fear of engulfment. Your confidence also helps you to expose your *true self* because you are not crippled by a fear of abandonment. Revealing your true self enhances intimacy potential. When you are self-confident, you are not threatened by others. Not being threatened by others allows you to *encourage* your spouse's spiritual growth.

It is *not* easy when his needs, are in conflict with yours.... When there is a challenge to resolve regarding opposing needs, strive to have the RELATIONSHIP win.

You will NOT succeed in a healthy and loving relationship unless ... BOTH of you have achieved self-love.

Almost always ... an intimacy deficient relationship is rooted in a lack of Self-Love.

Beware of the "twin bed syndrome." ... Remember when you first began dating you were deliriously happy when both of you shared a twin bed? As the relationship progressed you "graduated" to a full or queen size bed. By the time you married you were pondering a king. If you are considering twins again (but now you each want your own bed), or worse ... one of you wants to move to the guest room under the guise of being kept awake by snoring or other equally disturbing sleeping behaviors, a red flag is waving. If you do not heed the warning, you may end up in divorce court. Illness and advanced age intolerance can create exceptions; however, it is important to investigate the reasons for bed arrangement modifications in order to rule out marital stresses that have not yet surfaced.

133

"YOU-HE-WE"

In a healthy and loving marriage three "beings" need to co-exist ... you, he, we. If *any* of them is missing or not adequately nourished, your relationship will not thrive.

When conflicts arise ... the goal is for the "We" entity (relationship) to win.

EARLY MARRIAGE LOVE

Being "in love" feels like getting hit by a sledgehammer. Having "real love" feels like a gentle breeze on a starlit night.... Many people grieve when the "in love" stage vanishes. Some even end the relationship. Separation is a mistake, because the "in love" stage eventually fades from EVERY romantic relationship. Separation is also an error because it precludes *real* love from developing. Those that part as a result of "falling out of love" are doomed to serial marriages. If you have a history of leaving (physically or emotionally) when the "bloom fades," you may want to consider whether you could be addicted to drama and/or fear achieving true commitment and intimacy. If you have a history of being left at this stage, you may want to consider why you continue to be attracted to the "commitment phobics" and/or "drama addicts."

A frequent occurrence in early marriages ... is that one partner suddenly falls out of love and becomes panicked that he/she has married the wrong person. This is because we have been raised to believe that TRUE LOVE feels like fireworks. This is a MYTH. Real love begins to develop when the heat lowers and each has the opportunity to discover who the REAL, as opposed to FANTASY, person *actually* is.

Many couples "fall asleep" soon after they tie the knot.... They believe that marriage is the goal and once it has been reached, they may rest. This could not be further from the truth. The *only* way to sustain a viable relationship is through *regular* attention. If you are one of those who "fell asleep," wake up! ... and stay awake. If he has fallen asleep, wake him up. If he ignores your nudge, tell him that you are concerned about the perils of a "slumbering marriage."

Don't let yourself "go" because you are now married.... Not only are you doing a disservice to the marriage, but more importantly you are doing damage to YOURSELF!

THE BIG THREE

The Big Three: ... The most frequently cited issues of contention in marriages are: Money - Sex - Family (parents, in-laws, children, stepchildren). Without a solid communication base in which these *ongoing* challenges may be negotiated, any of these conflicts are capable of transporting the couple to divorce court.

It is not preordained that you will end up in divorce court or living in an unhappy marriage.... Marriage has been given a "bum rap" in today's society. It is true that many couples who are blissful at the altar end up divorced. However, this is not a product of the times, but rather an outcome of those unprepared for the "institution" of marriage. Successful relationships are not instinctual; they demand knowledge, skill, motivation, and a positive attitude. Do not "buy" into society's philosophy. If you do, you are doomed to become a statistic.

"CONTINUING EDUCATION" AND RECREATION TIME

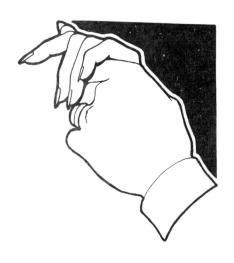

Allocate energy, time, and money to Relationship "Continuing Education." ... It does not matter whether it is an "individual growth seminar" that you attend jointly or a "couple's retreat." What is vital is that you resolve, together, to be mindful of the relationship in an active way. Appropriating time from the "regular" routine, as well as spending money on the event, conveys a message of importance regarding the priority of your commitment.

Put Recreation Time on your list of priorities.... You had time for it before you married. Make time for it now.

There are four distinctly different types of Recreation Time needed to keep your marriage unit intact ... individual, couple, family (if you have kids), and social. They are NOT to be combined! If any of these categories are compromised, the marriage is in jeopardy.

Couple Recreation time ... is to include *only* the two of you, no friends. "Recharging" the "couple battery" is imperative. When this vital battery is not recharged, it runs low (like any other battery) and finally dies!

Social Recreation time ... includes multiple options such as, the two of you getting together with other couples, in which there are no children present; your family playing with other families; relatives from both sides of your family; and/or a combination of families, relatives, and friends. Social recreation time indulges the human need to belong to a community.

You cannot have a successful family if you do not have a successful partnership.... The most important cog in the family wheel is the couple. If the couple is dysfunctional, the children will be too! If you "forget" or don't insist upon "couple time," the couple will eventually become dysfunctional.

If either partner is dysfunctional ... the couple will be dysfunctional.

SCHEDULED "CHECK-INS"

Incorporate into your routine, a structured way to *regularly* "check in." ... A "check-in" is an exercise in which you allocate time, energy, and attention to "listening and talking." You listen to what he shares with you and you tell him what is happening on your docket. The "check-in" serves as a way to stay "current" with each other both practically (who will pick up the milk on the way home from work) and emotionally. If you need help setting up a structured way to "check in," pick up a copy of *The Couples Companion: Meditations and Exercises for Getting the Love You Want*, by Harville Hendrix, Ph.D., and Helen Hunt, M.A., or *Passage to Intimacy*, by Lori H. Gordon, Ph.D., in which "The Daily Temperature Reading," an excellent technique developed by Virginia Satir for setting up effective communication, is explained. (See exercise section.)

The most frequent "check-in" traps: ...

- Couples do not schedule into their routines a *regular* time in which to do the "check-in" (each morning before getting out of bed; Monday, Wednesday, Saturday, and Sunday at dinner or before retiring...). Do not exercise a "laissez-faire" attitude; it will *not* get done.

- Couples spend longer than whatever time they have *allotted* for the "check-in" *on a particular day* (usually dealing with a conflict). This results in a hesitancy to do the exercise in the future when time is limited. Set your boundaries and respect them. Do *not* exceed the time you designate per "session."

- Couples begin to argue about a complaint *during* the "check-in" time as opposed to setting up an appointment, for *another time*, to deal with the issue. Consequently, negative feelings regarding "check-ins" are established since time boundaries are not being respected and complaints are allowed to "contaminate" the true purpose of "check-ins." When there is a complaint, indicate that you have one during the "check-in" and set aside a designated time to deal with it when *both* of you are available to give the issue proper attention and care.

- Couples do not use the technique as a *regular* way to "stay in touch" and *only* request the "check-in" when one has a complaint. Do not give into this temptation. It will end in a negative association with the exercise. Remember that the *purpose* of the "check-in" is to know what is going on with your partner, practically, emotionally, physically, and spiritually, not to complain.

HOUSEHOLD RESPONSIBILITIES

Household Duties can be a source of great tension.... Resolve that when both of you are employed full-time (staying at home to raise children is considered a full-time job), household duties will be equally shared! It is a good idea to practice role reversals of the "traditional tasks." For example, you mow the lawn, take the cars in for service, and dump the garbage. He cooks, does the laundry, and takes the kids to school. It is also effective to switch tasks. This allows for learning all the chores, so "pinch hitting" is easy. If one person experiences that the other is not carrying his/her fair share, resentment WILL build. A relationship with unresolved resentments will become toxic.

Do not overlook the possibility that tension around household management ... could *really* be a cover for some other unspoken and/or unresolved issue.

It is a good idea to give him a *choice* (as opposed to "an assignment") of which household tasks he will be responsible for.... Most people perform their jobs more efficiently when they feel as though they have been given options.

It is *unwise* to "go over his work." ... Once it is his responsibility, he needs to be able to do it *his own way*.

Don't hesitate to stray from the traditional stereotyped gender roles.... If he wants to sign up for "Cooking 101" and you are interested in "Auto Mechanics," indulge! It will promote flexibility and enrich the marriage.

"Neat-niks" and "slobs" CAN peacefully co-exist.... It is important to recognize that he was a slob (or neat-nik) before you met him. What is in our nature is not easily changed. What is modifiable is the *behavior* associated with the natural response. Start very early in the relationship (when all is new and you are still working at impressing each other) addressing your differences and making rules by which you are each willing to live regarding your respective "comfort zones." You may want to designate spaces in the house in which you each fully "enjoy your natures" where neither may criticize the other. The rest of the living area becomes a territory of negotiation in which you each *stretch* to accommodate the other. If these rules are not respected, they may become great sources of conflict and tension as the relationship matures.

If the "neat-nik/slob" behaviors become exaggerated ... this could be a sign that one of you is having a personal crisis or that something is wrong in the relationship. Do not ignore this behavior change; make an appointment to talk about it.

SEX IN MARRIAGE

A couple may have Sex without Love, and Love without Sex ... however, a healthy and loving marriage includes BOTH!

Sex and sexual intercourse are NOT interchangeable terms.... There may be times in the relationship when penetration is not possible. This is NOT a license to stop sexual activity.

When one partner wants sex and the other doesn't ... "servicing" (sexual release for one partner) may be an acceptable solution. Participation in this act fosters a loving and caring attitude toward the other without a compromise of self.

Age and certain medications may affect the sexual relationship.... This is *not* a prescription to stop! Explore the reasons for the shift.

Diminished sexual desire, male impotency, and difficulty achieving orgasm may be side effects of certain medications.... If this occurs, tell your doctor and insist on experimenting with other drugs.

If you are *not* on any prescription drug and notice a loss of sexual desire ... see a doctor. If no physical causes are found, a decrease in sexual interest is usually reflecting a problem in the relationship. However, there are circumstances in which this is not the case, such as psychological disorders or conflicts (depression, anxiety, low self-esteem, body changes resulting in body image distress); situational (grief reaction, job crisis), or developmental (age-related) transitions.

If you are having physical pain during sexual intercourse ...
consult a physician.

**Postmenopausal women may notice a diminished capacity
to lubricate during sexual arousal....** Hormone Replacement
Therapy (investigate this with your Ob-Gyn), as well as
over-the-counter lubricants may instantly fix the problem.

**If one of you has had surgery and/or suffers from a chronic
disease ...** do NOT hesitate to consult with your physician
regarding adaptations needed in your sexual relationship.

Sexual patterns *do* shift with age ... however, they need not
fade. If you and/or your partner are over fifty, begin reading
about physical changes that occur with age and how to adjust to
them.

Loss of sexual desire is NOT part of the aging process.... If it
occurs, have the courage to find out why!

TRUTH AND LIES

**It is often in our primary relationship that we have the
hardest time telling the truth ...** because it is in that
relationship that we have the most to lose. Yet, each time we
refrain from truth telling, we are taking a step away from
intimacy potential. Learning to tell the truth occurs when
self-love is high enough to KNOW you will survive and
eventually even thrive if he rejects you or leaves you because he
doesn't like your truths.

There are instances in which some thoughts, feelings, or experiences are better left unsaid or even denied.... Whether or not the person who is being told the secret *really* wants/needs to know, as well as who the secret is *really* protecting, generally reveals clues regarding whether it need be disclosed.

Before sharing or withholding a secret ... examine your integrity and your intentions.

There are many purposes for keeping secrets.... When you are keeping one, take the time to discover your reason.

People usually keep secrets ... because of an underlying fear.

Beware of "hidden agendas" in truth telling.... Sometimes we use truth telling as a means of revenge. Our intentions are not honest. If he is doing this, make him aware, and if he doesn't stop, dump him. If you are partaking, STOP. This path of truth telling is a form of self and relationship destruction.

The general rule of thumb regarding delivery of a truth:
1. Make sure you are sharing a truth with the correct intention.
2. Ask him if he wants and is ready to hear it. If he tells you he does *not* want to hear it, check out your integrity to determine whether he *needs* to know.
3. Deliver the news in the way in which *you* would want to hear a difficult truth.
4. Apply kindness, respect, and tact.

Omission is still a lie.... The *intentional* decision to withhold information even though you were not asked specifically about it is still a betrayal.

AFFAIRS

Since affairs tend to put the marriage at great risk ... if one is discovered and/or confessed, it is generally advisable to seek professional help.

Should affairs be confessed? ... There is continuing controversy in the mental health profession over whether to share affairs. And, there are always "exceptions to the rule" regarding whether or not to share an affair. That said ... if the affair is *ongoing and current,* no progression out of the

 quagmire of the primary relationship can be made until the affair is terminated. The termination of an ongoing and current affair will involve grief and a grief reaction will affect the primary relationship. The affair needs to be shared for this reason, as well as to confirm the suspicions of the other partner who knew something was wrong but did not know what. If the

affair happened in the *distant past*, is fully terminated, and is not a pattern in the relationship, this is usually one of those secrets that is better left unsaid. Examine your *intention* if you choose to share a past indiscretion. If you are sharing to rid yourself of guilt, *don't* share. *Your* guilt is *not* your partner's problem. If you are sharing from a position of courage, knowing that the affair is a block hindering the relationship, it needs to be shared. The expectation and prescription of complete honesty required in order to maintain a healthy and loving relationship versus whether all affairs, past and present, consummated and unconsummated, need be shared continues to be a difficult

145

paradox to reckon with. Since affairs can be so devastating , if you are not certain regarding your intention, seek the guidance of a therapist. (Remember to ask the therapist's bias with respect to admitting affairs.)

An undiscovered, ongoing affair ... is undermining the primary relationship. This includes unconsummated affairs, which can sometimes become even more potent than the consummated ones! (Fantasy is usually grander than reality!)

A "one-night stand" is not to be minimized.... It could cost you your physical and/or emotional health as well as your primary relationship.

Does a "one-night stand" need to be shared? ... Examine your motivations. If it is a confession, and not a pattern in the relationship, except (and this is a BIG except) for the physical health risk in which you have compromised your partner, don't share. Obviously, if you resist the temptation, you need not contend with this extraordinary issue. Whether to share or not to share is an issue that may be agreed upon *prior* to its occurrence. Those in healthy relationships acknowledge that bad things happen and negotiate strategies to get through them *before* the emotional toll wreaks havoc.

Affairs tend to either "make or break" the relationship.... When an affair occurs and is discovered, it tends to explode the relationship into a mosaic of bits. The mosaic may either be successfully glued into something even more beautiful than the whole before it shattered, or it remains in pieces. If it resides in "scraps," you may want to consider the viability of the relationship. If the relationship is successfully renewed, remember that it will take TIME for the betrayed to trust and respect again.

If you are still examining his collars for lipstick, smelling his clothes for perfume, and checking his pockets, briefcase, phone bills, and credit card receipts a year later ... you may want to consider the viability of the relationship.

If the relationship survives the affair ... it is important to understand what made the "indiscretion" happen so as to prevent a reoccurrence. Seek professional help if you are unsuccessful at achieving this task.

BETRAYALS AND FORGIVENESS

Forgiving and Forgetting are NOT interchangeable concepts.... You will never forget a betrayal, but it is within your power to forgive it.

An act which has not been forgiven may take a major toll on *your* physical, emotional, and spiritual health.... It may even cost you your life!

When you have not forgiven the act ... you are in some way still being controlled by the person who committed the betrayal.

You do not need to excuse the act ... in order to forgive the person who betrayed you.

Deciding to forgive the betrayal does NOT mean you need to stay in the relationship.... No one but YOU can decide whether a betrayal will cost the relationship. What is non-negotiable for one may not be the case for another. This is not a matter of "right or wrong." This is a situation in which you need to discover what the best choice is for you.

Leaving the relationship because an act of betrayal has been committed ... is not the same as forgiving the person who committed it. Whether you leave or whether you stay, you must forgive the person who committed the act in order to maintain *your* physical, mental, and spiritual well-being.

When the choice is to *terminate* the relationship, the act of forgiveness ... is a "letting go" of him. He no longer "consumes" your thoughts, feelings, or behaviors. He has been released from your psyche, and you wish him well. Eventually, you no longer feel "stirred up" (sexual attraction, hatred, anger, sad, hurt) when you think about him or see him, and finally you feel indifferent.

When the choice is to *remain* in the relationship, the act of forgiveness ... is often more difficult to achieve, since the person who committed the betrayal is still present. Before deciding to stay, you *must* observe behaviors that clearly indicate he is ready to do *his* part to repair the fractured relationship. Next, be certain that your inner voice has told you to stay. Once you have concluded both of these "missions," achieving forgiveness begins with the *desire* to forgive. Following the desire comes the "action" (your behaviors), which is governed by your attitude. You need to decide *not* to keep "rerunning" the act out loud (to him) or in your head. As you practice your new behaviors, you may have to borrow the Alcoholics Anonymous slogan of : "Fake it until you make it." (In other words, you may have to *act as if* the anger, sadness, fear, hurt, and mistrust are gone.) Finally, opening your heart is a requirement. An opened heart renders you vulnerable and at great risk of hurt and loss once again; however, true healing cannot occur without it. Healing an injury is a slow process. Do not allow your periods of discouragement to dissuade you from your goal. It is vital that the betrayer understand that recovery *does* take time, and patience is called for when the betrayed slips. Slipping, however, does *not* include permission to punish, seek revenge, or abuse the betrayer. A betrayer is doing himself a major disservice if he allows any of these behaviors under the guise of guilt.

Sometimes forgiveness entails ... letting go of being the victim. For some, this letting go may be difficult since the "victim position" has been a lifestyle.

You *will* have intuitive clues after a betrayal regarding what to do with the relationship.... You will probably experience some or all of the following feelings and observations:

If there is hope ...
- Although you feel scared, you are also excited about the prospect of rebuilding the relationship.
- You feel relief.
- You *know* that he is highly motivated to do his part through observation of his behaviors.
- He recognizes that it will take time for him to earn your respect and trust again.
- Your body feels "happy."

If you need to move on ...
- The "brutal" inner voice may utter things like: "it's over, too late, get out, it's finished...."

- The "subtle" inner voice may jar memories such as a "snap" that occurred inside, upon discovery of the betrayal and a realization that suddenly you felt estranged and/or disconnected.
- You may uncover the stark reality that your love for him is gone.
- You may recognize a deep sadness and ferret out that you are grieving because something has died.
- Another possibility is that you discover that you will never trust or respect him again.
- You may have body sensations instead of thoughts, such as, the "thought" of "working it out" makes your stomach feel queasy; you feel dread at the cellular level; or you develop uncomfortable body symptoms that feel like an illness in which no cause is found.
- You may detect that he is not highly motivated to regain your trust and respect, and/or notice that he is not exerting much energy toward "gluing" the relationship back together.

If you were the "betrayer" ... it is imperative that you discover the reason you betrayed. Was it an opportunity to get out or a call for help. If you don't do your homework, you are "doomed" to betray again.

If you were the "betrayed" one ... it is important to look at what *your* role was in rendering the relationship vulnerable to betrayal. Betrayals do not usually occur in a vacuum. They are the result of a problem in the relationship in which one does the "acting out" by betraying. Just as it is vital to discover the reason you betrayed, it is also critical to learn your part as the "betrayed," because if you don't you are likely to find yourself in the same situation again.

You have not truly forgiven until you have ... constructively expressed your feelings surrounding the betrayal, recognized a strong desire to forgive, reconciled that the process takes time, practiced behavior changes, adjusted your attitudes, and opened your heart. These rules apply to "current" acts of betrayal as well as to childhood wounds. (See exercise section.)

KEEPING THE MARRIAGE INTERESTING

Don't neglect to continue surprising your husband with "unexpected gifts" ... whether it is a note in his briefcase, an invitation to an all-expenses-paid activity (that *he* will enjoy), or his favorite home cooked meal. These gestures are the ones that sustain the "juice" and carry you through the "hard times."

Do something (or give him something) that is *totally* out of character for you.... Keep him intrigued. Boredom hurts and can make certain people more susceptible to "wandering."

RETIREMENT

Retirement has a huge impact on the marriage regardless of which structure the family system has lived (one, both or neither working outside of the home).
Some of the scenarios ...

- "*You* are retiring, but *I* am off to work every day, business as usual."

- "*You* are retiring, but *I* am still performing all the household chores (cooking, cleaning, laundry), business as usual."

- "*I* am retiring, but *you* are off to work every day, business as usual."
- "Even though *you* have conducted your business in the home, you won't have your business to manage anymore."
- "Even though *I* have conducted my business in the home, I won't have my business to manage anymore."
- "Even though we have *both* conducted our businesses in the home, neither of us will have our respective businesses (or the same business) to manage anymore."
- "After years of *both* being employed full-time outside the home (at the same place of employment or different places of employment), we are both going to be home with time on our hands that we have not had since the courtship."

There are some consistent challenges that run through each scenario and there are issues particular to each. The most important thing to remember is that there *will be* shifts as a result of this life transition and that these changes need to be addressed and worked through in order to maintain a healthy and loving relationship.

This stage of life may either be a renewal period or a time of great stress.... It may be a renewal period because responsibilities have lessened considerably, the children are out of the home, and more time is available to realize the wishes, hopes, and dreams that have been in place since early in the marriage. It may be a time of great stress if differences which have been "ignored" previously (because of hectic schedules, parenting, etc.) now become exaggerated (because of more time together) and not resolved.

No matter how happy the retiree may be regarding finally arriving at this stage of life ... there will be a grief reaction once he "lets in" that his working career is over. Do not be surprised if he suffers a bout of depression. He may also experience anger, anxiety, unexplained somatic (physical) symptoms, malaise, insomnia, fatigue, lessened energy, forgetfulness, indecisiveness, concentration difficulties, and/or a general feeling of "losing his mind." Just about "anything goes" when a person is grieving. The same applies to you if you are the retiree.

Expect that the nonworking (or nonretiring) spouse ... will also have some major adjustment reactions at this life stage.

There could be diminished physical capacities ... yet another loss to reckon with.

What people do not realize is that ... there is a grief reaction resulting from *any* loss, even "happy losses" such as a move (leaving behind the old neighborhood), the birth of a child (never again only the couple), or the departure of a child to college (the empty nest). Consequently, even if the retired couple is truly happy about finally arriving at this stage of life, there will be a grief response.

One of the errors made by couples who arrive at this stage of life is ... not fully recognizing that it is time to re-negotiate the roles that applied in the "working" years but are presently obsolete.

Even if *you* are not close to this stage of life ... your parents are. Recognize that they may be going through some of these major overhauls. It is not your business to interfere. Let them work it out.

LAUGHTER

LAUGHTER ... serves a different and necessary purpose in each stage of relationship building. Not only is it *bonding*, but it is very difficult to laugh and stay angry at the same time. It breaks down barriers, releases tension, and improves body function. Laughter makes your heart and spirit smile. It offers reprieves from this difficult, scary and painful life. If you have been blessed with the ability to laugh at yourself and with others, be grateful. If you don't laugh much, begin practicing!

Laughter is great medicine.... During the hunt phase, you need humor to endure the difficult *moments*. During commitment and marriage, you need humor to endure the difficult *times*.

Blessed moments occur ... if you and your partner can share belly laughs together. Relish the gift. It is with only a few in your lifetime that you will experience this pleasure.

DEATH

A topic often avoided is discussion of death.... It's going to happen. Not discussing it does NOT delay it. Your spouse is the best person with whom to share your wishes. Being young does not protect you from the inescapable. Include in these discussions living will requests. Also explore with each other how much and what you each want to be told regarding "terminal illness" should either of you become afflicted.

Draw up a will.... Being young does not preclude a sudden death.

Draw up a *living* will.... It is MUCH harder for your spouse to follow through with your wishes if you do not have a legal document.

When one of your parents loses his/her spouse ... let your remaining parent survive the grief in the manner in which appears most comfortable for him/her. The baby boomer generation is the first to emphasize dealing with sorrow openly. Don't judge if he/she decides to re-couple (or remarry) very quickly after the loss of *your* parent. A rapid re-coupling is *not* a slight against you or your deceased parent; it is simply gratifying a need that you as the child are unable to fulfill.

***Hopefully,* the issue of where an elderly remaining parent will reside ...** has been resolved long before the occurrence of either parent's death. If this is *not* the case, skillful negotiation of this question is important and requires careful processing since the decision will dramatically affect all of the parties involved.

The death of one parent does *not* mean ... it is time to step in and take over your remaining parent's life.

MARRIAGE FAILURE

The fact is that most marriages fail because couples never uncover and *heal* the hidden aspects of the relationship.... Examples of hidden aspects include such things as childhood wishes, hopes, dreams, expectations, and wounds.

Most couples fail with professional help ... because they seek it too late.

Another high cause of divorce ... is that couples do not learn the skills necessary in order to succeed in a healthy and loving relationship.

If you decide to separate even if you think there is a good chance you will reconcile ... have a *legal property settlement* drawn up, before you physically part. Making sure your legal affairs are in order prior to the separation prevents unexpected emotional flare-ups or unintentional betrayals from interfering with working out reasonable (fair) property settlement negotiations.

If you resolve to separate in a less prudent fashion concluding that you do not need to draw up a property settlement ... at the very least establish *out loud*, ground rules such as whether dating and/or sleeping with others is allowed. Never a s s u m e that you are each living by the same separation rules. The most frequent cause of blowups during trial separations (which end up in divorce court) is the violation of an *unspoken* agreement on the part of one party, resulting in the other feeling betrayed since that party had a different *assumption* and/or expectation.

Most property settlements automatically contain a clause permitting socialization (including sex) with parties outside the marriage.... If you do *not* want to sanction dating and/or sleeping with others during your separation, make those requests explicit and be certain that your partner has agreed.

In most states, if you get back together, a property settlement becomes null and void since it has not progressed to divorce court.... However, the most judicious thing to do if you fall into this category is to contact an attorney (practicing in the state in which you would file for divorce), to be sure that this is the case.

If you decide to file for divorce ... seek a mediator (as opposed to separate attorneys)! It will save you an *enormous* amount of money and your emotional distress will be significantly diminished. By definition, when you each have an attorney, you *will* become polarized. This is because the attorney's job is to get the *best* possible settlement for his or her client. In order to satisfy this mission, the attorney must "rob" the other party of assets and custodial arrangements. If the two

 of you are so bitter that the attorneys must do the negotiating, each time they speak on the phone, work up documents, etc., you will receive another bill. A mediator represents *both* of you and therefore is most successful at his

business when you are *both* satisfied. In mediation, each emerges a winner. With separate attorneys, there is usually a winner and a loser (and it is often the wife who loses). Even for the winner, however, frequently a tremendous amount of money has been spent and the emotional toll on him and the children is not worth it.

Mediators come in two genres: ... "mental health practitioner" and "attorney." Select the attorney type. You may forego great mental health counseling skills, but in this circumstance, you have sought professional help to make you fully aware of your state's divorce laws. An attorney's job is to know these laws. If you need the emotional counsel, spend the extra money and get a psychotherapist.

There may be certain exceptions in which seeking separate legal counsel is the only alternative.... For example, you may feel too depleted or too defeated to guard what is rightfully and legally yours.

FINAL REMINDER

Finally, remember ... that, although this book includes many ideas, it is up to you to examine them, retain them, or spit them out. An area as extensive as searching for, selecting, and maintaining a healthy and loving relationship cannot be covered comprehensively in any guide. There are exceptions to all rules. What is so exciting about the human condition is its mystery, which by definition means that "nothing is steadfast." You, and *only* you, can decide which nuggets "fit" and which are meant for others. Good Luck!

LAST NUGGET

Most important of all, apply these nuggets ... to ANY significant relationship you are interested in finding and keeping (whether it be with yourself, your friend, your lover, your husband, your siblings, your parents, your children, your relatives, his relatives, your employer, your employee, your co-worker, your neighbor, your doctor, your therapist, your lawyer, even your Indian chief!) The rules vary slightly depending on the genre of relationship. For example, relationships that are bestowed on you (meaning you do not choose them, such as your parents, your siblings, your children,

or his relatives), may require more "leeway" since you may wish to keep these people in your life, even if they are unwilling to do their part to sustain a loving and healthy relationship. Under no circumstances, however, are you to compromise yourself! Some situations such as an abusive marriage require termination or professional help in order to achieve "health." Family bonds are only to be "cut off" as a LAST resort, after everything else has failed. In short, these nuggets are guidelines to help you find, select, and sustain loving and healthy relationships with others and most critically with yourself. Once you discover who your *true* self is and learn to love and respect her (which you accomplish by being involved with others), you will master not jeopardizing her in *any* way. As each of us learns to grow, change, and LOVE, the planet becomes a better place to BE. Knowledge (awareness), Power, and Love all begin with one (the self). Happy preparing, happy hunting, happy working, and happy keeping!

EXERCISES

If you are interested in going beyond an intellectual understanding of the nuggets ... this section is devoted to *concrete* things that you may do to improve your odds in preparing, hunting, deciding, keeping, committing, and marrying.

Uncensored **writing ...** explores, discovers, purges, and heals. A pen in hand can reach the unconscious, often accessing unexpected and unknown information. Once you claim this information, you can begin the process of healing yourself. The key is to write "for your eyes only." Once you begin to edit, you cease to be on the pathway of the unconscious. If you are writing something with the intention of giving it to someone, write it *first* to yourself. Then, after you have completed your own letter, revise it for the other person. Do *not* skip the first draft (the *unedited* version), in an attempt to save time. You will have missed the purpose of the exercise.

Keep a journal.... The reasons for a journal are specific to each individual who keeps one. You might write ...

- To observe your process of self-discovery and spiritual growth.
- To see from whence you've come years or even months ago.
- To record your thoughts, feelings, and behaviors.
- To note insights regarding your thoughts, feelings, and behaviors.
- To notice whether your beliefs, attitudes, and values are changing.
- To record your waking, as well as your sleeping, dreams.

- To write your aspirations, wishes, and life goals.
- To dialogue with yourself (writing about the issue from differing points of view) regarding questions and conflicts.
- To monitor your relationships with others, especially your partner.

Since *married* and *partnered* women will be doing exercises in areas other than the Commitment and Marriage section, the option of choosing the spouse or partner as a "coach" is included when exercises call for the use of assistants.

GETTING PREPARED

Affirmations ... Create your own affirmations and say them to yourself at least 100 times a day. Write as many as you can come up with in your journal and say a different one daily. Keep them "short and sweet." If there is an affirmation in particular that speaks to you, stay with it until you feel ready to begin with another. Examples:

- "I deserve Love and Respect."
- "I take care of myself first."
- "I love myself first."
- "I AM."
- "I am unique."
- "I am beautiful."
- "I love my body."
- "God loves me."
- "I will survive and even thrive."

- "I am free!"
- "I am safe."
- "I have inner strength."
- "I am powerful!"
- "I can let go."
- "I am good enough." *
- "I am lovable." *
- "It is *not* against you.... It is for me." *
- "I am in charge of me." *
- "My best is good enough." *
- "I don't *need* you." *
- "I won't let you use me." *
- "I'm entitled to make mistakes." *
- "I'm entitled to be happy." *
- "No!" *
- "I'm afraid, but I'll do it anyway." *
- "I'm responsible for my behavior." *

* Thank you, Lori Gordon, Ph.D., founder of "PAIRS," (Practical Application of Intimate Relationship Skills) for lending these affirmations. PAIRS Training Manual and Curriculum Guide, Vol. II, 1992, rev.7/95, p. 394.

Relaxation Exercises ... diaphragm breathing, deep muscle relaxation, visualization ... There are many ways to get relaxed. I have listed three. Try each one to see which is most appealing to you. If you have a particular interest, there are many books dedicated to both relaxation and meditation (which are not interchangeable).

The optimal recommendation for the relaxation exercise is 20 minutes *twice* a day. Since many of you will not put aside that amount of time, set a realistic goal and *commit* to it. Five minutes twice a day or ten minutes once a day is certainly better than nothing at all.

In each situation, begin by getting in a comfortable position, sitting or lying down. (You may be vulnerable to falling asleep in the prone position.) Many people close their eyes, but it is not necessary.

Diaphragm breathing ... Begin by simply noticing your breathing. Once you have settled down, start to breathe from your diaphragm. The easy way to know if you are breathing from your diaphragm is to put your hand on your abdomen and breathe until you are successful at expanding the area fully with each incoming breath. Breathe slowly and mindfully. There are infinite breathing techniques. Here are two very simple ones:

1. **"Breathing in fours"** ... When you are learning this breathing technique, repeat the process five times. As you become more experienced increase your "reps" to ten times or as many as you can comfortably achieve.

As slowly as possible, count to four as you are breathing in, hold your breath for four counts and count to four while you are breathing out. After you have completed the "reps," sit quietly for the remaining time and focus on your usual breathing pattern. If your natural rhythm is *not* diaphragm style, strive to become a natural diaphragm breather.

2. Breathing with words ... As you breathe *in*, silently say a word that evokes calmness such as Love, Peace, Light, Calm, Relax. As you breathe *out*, silently say a word that elicits a negative sensation, such as Fear, Tension, Stress. Or, you might want to expand your words into sentences, saying, "I am breathing *in* Peace" as you inhale, and "I am breathing *out* Fear," as you exhale. Other sentence pairs might be: "I am letting in Love" / "I am letting go of Tension"; or "I am feeling Calm" / "I am letting go of Fear." Come up with a formula that works for you, focusing on the positive feelings as you *in*hale and negative feelings as you *ex*hale.

When possible, breathe through your nose.

Many people are "chest breathers." In states of fear, this form of shallow breathing tends to accelerate anxiety.

Deep muscle relaxation.... Before you begin to practice the deep muscle relaxation, spend a few minutes focusing on your breathing. Do several "breathing in fours," or just sit quietly and concentrate on your natural breathing rhythm.

There are two simple ways to practice releasing tense muscles:

1. **Focus on the area that you want to relax....** Constrict those muscles and hold them tightened for a few seconds, then release them.

2. **Focus on the area that you want to relax ...** and release it. This format omits the tensing of the muscle area before releasing it.

Start with your skull or forehead and progress through all your face areas, eyes, nose, cheeks, mouth, jaw, chin, ears, neck (front and back), shoulders, chest, abdomen, upper back, lower back, right arm to fingertips, left arm to fingertips, pelvis, genitals, buttocks, right leg to toes, left leg to toes. You may begin from your toes and proceed to your head if that feels more comfortable. Move through the exercise as slowly as you can.

Visualization ... Before you begin with the image, spend a few minutes paying attention to your breathing pattern. When you feel ready, visualize a place in nature or *anywhere* (a room, a bed, a place you have been or a place you conjure up) and make it *your* sanctuary ... a place where no one comes uninvited. Activate all your senses. What do you see, smell, hear, touch, taste? If you are outside, what is the temperature, is it sunny or overcast, day or night? Put yourself in that place and stay there for as long as you are able. The more deeply you can stimulate your senses in the image, by savoring colors, forms, and textures; and by identifying odors, sounds, and sensations, the more successful at the relaxation experience you will be.

Letting Go of Perfection ... It is very exhausting to be PERFECT, and not good for your physical, emotional, and spiritual well-being. *Your best is good enough.* If you are a PERFECTIONIST and you want to let go of this trait, pick a few things you can work on to practice being less perfect. For example:

- If you are a "neat-nik," leave the house for the day with dishes in the sink, an unmade bed, and dirty clothes piled on top of the washer.
- If you need to have your makeup on before you leave the house, go out without your "mask."
- If you are compelled to be on time, arrive late for work.

If you never take sick days, call in sick, stay home and watch soap operas or go to the mall....

Before you can truly let go of your perfectionism characteristic, you will need to stretch your behaviors in the opposite direction a little beyond where you would normally be comfortable. This is why there are some "extreme" circumstances in this exercise such as being late for work or calling in sick. The key to your success is *regular practice*. An occasional "attempt" to be less perfect will *not* change the behavior.

Pick at least one thing per week over the next few weeks that you typically need to be perfect about and do it less perfectly. Write about what you anticipate will happen and how you will feel doing your less-than-perfect thing. After you have done your exercise, write about how it felt to do it and how you feel now.

How to Accomplish a Goal ... If, for example, you determine that walking three times a week will improve your self-love, make this a goal.

1. Declare it out loud and write it in your journal. " I will walk three times a week."

2. Set a date to begin.

3. Set a date to assess your progress.

4. Make it measurable (walking three times a week can be measured). Abstract goals such as "I want to love myself" or "I want to be happy" are too difficult to assess.

5. At assessment time, ask yourself if you accomplished the goal. If you have, do you want to establish a new goal, or do you want to continue working on the same one? If you have not, how do you need to revise it? For example, you may decide to rise an hour earlier. Ask yourself whether the original goal was attainable and realistic. Were you truly motivated? Were you sabotaging your progress? If so, how?

6. Set a new starting date.

7. Set a new assessment date.

8. Be kind to yourself. Remember that you *will* slip. Pick yourself up, brush yourself off, and begin again.

Self-Love Goals List ... If you are having difficulty creating a self-love goals list, imagine that one of your friends (pick a real person) has asked you to help make up her self-love goals list. What hints do you give her regarding the sorts of actions, thoughts, and feelings she would possess *if* she loved herself? In what ways do you encourage her to treat herself *if* she loved herself? What are her priorities? What are her values? The answers to these questions are items to put on *your* self-love goals list.

Another way to help you get started with your list is to think about someone you admire and respect who you believe loves herself. What does she do and say that leads you to believe that she values, loves, and respects herself?

If you are still unclear about what needs to be on your list, write down, without thinking too much about it, what you believe to be the ten most important criteria in successful parenting. These criteria become your "self-love goals" list. Why this suggestion? Because you are in effect "re-parenting yourself" and a paramount component of successful parenting teaches self-love.

Repairing the Damage of the Past ... If you have the courage, ask a coach (spouse, partner, trusted friend, or psychotherapist) to come along for the ride. It absolutely does aid in the healing process. Select a time, in which you will have no interruptions and no clock deadlines, so you may go "wherever you need to go."

1. In a relaxed state, revisit the scene of the trauma.

2. Reframe the trauma by *replacing* what *actually* happened with an image of what you would have wished for.

3. Say out loud what is happening or have the experience silently. (A silent visualization tends to intensify feelings.)

4. If you have a coach along, role play the person who wounded you and say out loud to your inner child, for the coach to witness, exactly what you would have wanted to hear. If you prefer, ask the coach to become the person who wounded you and have him/her say to you what you would have wished for.

5. If you have no coach, look yourself in the mirror and say out loud the things you would have liked to have heard.

6. In cases where violent acts were committed, you may want to visualize yourself becoming a person, monster, or force larger and stronger than the "perpetrator" and in your newfound power, stopping him or her!

7. Or you may decide to write a letter to the person who hurt you. If you pick this option, it is very important to *also* write a "response letter" in which you include everything you would have wanted to hear. Read the response letter out loud, or more powerful still, have another person read it to you.

8. Whatever method of repair you choose, the final step is for the "parent" part of yourself to take over from your primary caretakers the *responsibility* for your inner child. You can now guarantee to her that such a happening will *never* occur again. You also have the power to change old beliefs ("Don't trust men.") into new beliefs ("Not all men are like my father. Some men are trustworthy."). What is done is done. It is time to heal yourself and get on with the business of living a healthy and loving life. Only you can make that choice. I urge you to take the risk.

9. After you have completed the exercise, take time with your journal to write your reflections. This is an important part of the process, since writing helps to integrate thoughts and feelings.

Letting Go of the Prince, (or Toad) ... If you are grieving and were not able to express all you had to say to your former Prince, (or Toad):

1. Settle in a comfortable chair with a box of tissues.

2. Take five s l o w breaths to help you relax and gently close your eyes.

3. When you feel ready ... see him in front of you and say silently (or out loud) everything you want him to hear. (Since he

isn't really there, let it all hang out, no matter how silly you feel.)

4. Imagine him responding. During that time, look into his eyes and "see" what he is *really* feeling. (Often when we look into someone's eyes, we see the sad and/or scared child who resides within, allowing us to feel more compassion toward that person.)

5. Continue with this dialogue until it has reached its natural conclusion.

6. Write reflections in your journal.

Releasing grudges ... Grudges are harming YOU much more than they are hurting the person or people you are "grudging."
Begin the exercise by:

1. Thinking about the person against whom you are holding a grudge.

2. Pull out your journal and start writing whatever comes to mind. Let it ALL HANG OUT. Be as "ugly" as you wish. Remember, no one will see this journal entry but you!

3. When you stop writing and you sit for a while and nothing else comes to mind, reread what you have written. All four feelings (Mad, Sad, Glad, Scared) should be on the paper. If they are NOT, stay with the exercise until they are. Often the hardest part is to come up with what you are glad about.

4. Spend a few moments writing about how it felt to do the exercise. Do you feel any less grudging? Any surprises? Did you learn anything? Sometimes a surprise is the discovery of one's own guilt, regret, shame, or responsibility regarding the behavior which created the grudge.

If you would like to intensify the experience:

5. Write a response letter to your exercise. This letter would be from the person against whom you hold the grudge. Include EVERYTHING you would like to hear.

6. Have someone you trust read the response letter to you. If this is not an option, read it *out loud* to yourself.

7. Write your reflections in your journal. What did you learn? How do you feel? Do you need to do the exercise again? Pick someone else (or the same person, another grudge) and do the exercise again.

If you decide that you would like to make contact with the "grudgee" by letter, write a "second draft" in which you include only that which is pertinent to him/her.

Releasing guilt ... Pick something you feel guilty about. Let yourself feel the underlying anger (and any other feelings) as well as your regret for the act (or non act) committed. Make amends if necessary and/or possible with others, and then, most importantly, forgive yourself! After you have allowed yourself to feel the feelings, write about the experience. Continue selecting situations in which you feel guilty and repeat the exercise. Letting go of guilt is a long and arduous process; do not be discouraged if you do not feel relieved each time you do the exercise. Resolve to continue practicing.

"Yeses and Noes" ... Say "yes" to something you would normally say "no" to (but secretly want to say "yes") and "no" to something you would normally say "yes" to (but secretly want to say "no")…. This exercise will get you on the road to expressing yourself more assertively. After you have done the exercise and spent time with your journal reflecting on how it felt to do it, start increasing your frequency and risk level of "yeses and noes."

Filling Up ... Take at least one hour out of each day, a *minimum* of three days a week, to do something that is *just* for you. During that period, do not answer the phone. If you are living with others, *insist* on NO interruptions. On your designated days, plan ahead to what you will do for that particular "time-out." You may choose a bubble bath, a stroll, reading a pleasure book, or you may decide that you just want to sit. The key is to *require* of *yourself*, and of all who know you, that taking your "time-out" is *as much a priority* as your other life responsibilities. Once you have successfully and *consistently* conveyed this message to yourself and to others, you will be surprised at how quickly those around you will be responsive and respectful of your "time-outs." If you have female children, modeling this behavior of "time-out for the self" is extremely important.

Pre-date Checklist ... Ask yourself: Am I ready to date? Do I look the way I want to look? Am I dressing to convey my true self, as opposed to what I think I am supposed to project? (Remember, it is a major time-saver to *begin* as your real self rather than to *become* your true self after you have met your prospect.) Am I clean? Do I smell nice? (If you can smell your own perfume, you probably have too much on.) Am I recalling what is important to me, my "bottom lines," my values, my priorities? Am I remembering not to become consumed with my external appearance at the expense of my true self? Do I have a positive attitude about dating? (If I don't, I will be wasting my time.) Have I acquired the ability to laugh at myself? (Dating does NOT have to be a serious venture. Comic relief is quite a stress reducer, and it is usually a much-needed ingredient for those venturing off into the dating world.) Am I ready to meet new people? Have I healed from past relationships? Would I want to date myself? And, finally, am I remembering to bring *myself* on the date? If you have forgotten to bring yourself ... stop whatever you are doing ... sit down ... smile ... and ... BREATHE!

HUNT AND "KEEPER" DATING CRITERIA CHECKLISTS

Things to keep in mind while working on:
- **1. The ABC's of Search, Selection, and Maintenance of the Relationship**

- **2. Ten Essential Characteristics**
- **3. Ideal Partnership**

- **There are NO right or wrong items to have on your checklists....** Do not let *anyone* sway you. Do not be bridled by the "expectations" of your culture. *You* are the person who will be with this man. You are the *only* one who can establish your list.
- **Do not limit your items ...** to external characteristics (level of education, level of income, height, build) or external life choices (non-smoker, pet owner).
- **Include on your list ...** societal, religious, political, spiritual, and philosophical views, willingness and ability to share feelings, and interest in personal growth.
- **Make sure ...** the list is specific and "measurable." (See "How to accomplish a goal," Exercise section, which explains "measurable.")
- **All the lists are in a constant state of flux....** One of the reasons to date lots of prospects is to determine which features continue to remain constant and which may be adjusted if he appears in other ways to be your Prince. Updating and fine-tuning these "ledgers" will ultimately help you become quite clear regarding your requirements and preferences. Stay open and flexible.

1. The ABC's of Search, Selection, and Maintenance of the Relationship ... When you are ready to begin the Hunt, pull out your journal and start with your ABC's. Pick as many words as you can conjure per letter, regarding either search, selection, or maintenance of the relationship. These words will serve as your guidelines. For example: **a**wareness ... **b**rave ... **c**ommit ... **c**are **d**esire ... **e**ffort ... **f**orgive ... **f**idelity ... **g**entle ... **h**eart ... **h**onest integrity ... judicious ... kind ... love ... mask ... negotiate ... other ... play ... quest ... responsible ... reliable ... spirit ... trust unconditional ... valiant ... work ... xanadu ... you ... zealous.

Whenever you think of another word, add it to your list. During your "quiet time," think about the words you selected, why you chose them, and why they are important to you. Which "guidelines" are mandatory and which would you be willing to forgo? Journal your reflections.

2. Ten Essential Characteristics ... Make a checklist of at least 10 essential characteristics that the Prince must embody, BEFORE you begin the hunt. When you are ready to "assess" him, if he doesn't possess *at least* 5 ... move on.

3. Ideal Partnership ... BEFORE the hunt, take quiet time (and journal time) to imagine your ideal partnership. Clearly see what you are doing. Notice what he is doing. What is each person's part in making the relationship successful and special? If a couple were to ask you what they needed to do in order to have as healthy and loving a relationship as yours, what would you say? It cannot be stressed enough that you need to complete this task *before* you begin the hunt, since you will not be objective regarding your "relationship requirements" if you have already met a possible "keeper."

THE HUNT

How to Respectfully and Tactfully Reject Others ... This is done in much the same way as the general rule of thumb for delivery of a truth (see Commitment and Marriage section, "Truth and Lies"). Refuse the person in the way in which *you* would want to be refused. Remain kind, tactful, and respectful.

Commitment to The Hunt ... When you are ready to begin the Hunt, commit to yourself that *at least once a week* you will actively pursue *some* element related to this undertaking. Examples:

- Tell one of your friends that you are ready to meet a prospective Prince.
- Decide to have a conversation with an attractive man (without a wedding band) in the produce section or check-out line at the grocery store.
- Attend some event that interests you, promising yourself that you will not be a wallflower.

"KEEPER" DATING

Connections between Thoughts and Feelings ... If you can successfully change your thoughts, your feelings will change. Notice what happens to your body when you view the same experience with a different thought process. For example:

Your feelings are hurt and you are angry because the Prince forgot your date. You are feeling sorry for yourself because you aren't important enough to be remembered. You are scared because you really like the guy and you are concluding that you may have to break up. You continue to work yourself into a frenzy until suddenly you remember that his dog was killed that day and part of what attracted you to him was his remarkable relationship with this animal. Notice what happens to your body when you recall this tragedy.

Sometimes you don't have the facts and you can opt to get upset or not. For example:

You are merrily driving along and a car cuts in front of you with no apparent regard for your presence. Your first reaction is to be overtaken with road rage and the only reason you aren't willing to do something equally unnerving to him is because you are afraid he has a gun.

Now, practice another reaction; entertain the thought that he may be having a very bad day because his child is critically ill. He simply was not paying attention and is eternally grateful that you were vigilant enough to prevent the accident. Hold that thought and notice the difference between the sensations in your body when you felt personally affronted versus when you allowed him compassion.

The Feeling Survey ... The purpose of this exercise is to discover what you are feeling. You cannot effectively communicate your feelings if you do not know them.

Spend several weeks in which, a minimum of 20 times each day, you stop whatever you are doing for 30 seconds and ask yourself whether you are mad, sad, glad, scared, derivative, ambivalent or a combination of these feelings. Remember that often underneath the safe feelings are the hidden (real) feelings. (Derivative, ambivalent, combination, hidden and safe feelings are explained in the "Feelings" section of "Keeper" Dating.)

If you want to learn what feeling you spend the majority of your time with, carry a 3x5 card and mark your answer each time you ask yourself the question. Many people are surprised with their discovery.

Paraphrasing ... Practice paraphrasing *regularly*. During the "Keeper" Dating phase, couples are less likely to set prescribed times to "check-in" with each other. However, since the rules that you will live by are etched in granite by the time you are married, it is a good idea to establish the habit of customary "check-ins" early in the relationship.

Create certain "check-ins," in which you *routinely* paraphrase with each other. Like learning any other skill, the more you do it, the better you become. When you are both adept at paraphrasing you may comfortably use this method when you are struggling with an issue and need to be able to *correctly* understand each other's position. If you practice paraphrasing *only* when you are stressed, you will be unsuccessful. (Paraphrasing is explained in the "Communication" section of "Keeper" Dating.)

Caring ... List a minimum of 10 things that your partner could do for you that would make you feel cared about. Have him do the same and then exchange the lists. Commit to each other that you will regularly grant requests on your respective lists. Periodically, check in with each other to get your scores. Be sure to make these caring acts *measurable* (I would like him to make dinner for me twice a week) as opposed to vague, (I wish he would be more loving). When wishes are measurable, they are achievable. When they are vague, they are doomed to fail.

Boundary Mindfulness ... means to be conscious at all times of *your* boundaries and *everyone else's*. Do not let anyone come into your "sandbox" uninvited and do not jump into anyone else's without permission. (See "Boundaries," "Keeper" Dating section for sandbox explanation.) The only way you will become proficient with this "requirement" for healthy and loving relationships, is if you *practice consistent* boundary respect. Teach those with whom you are close (your prospective Prince, your kids, your family of origin, your friends ...) about the "sandbox concept" and ask them to alert you if you slip, whether it be intruding into their space or allowing them to come into yours without an invitation.

In a partnership, having the understanding that you will each say: "You have jumped into my sandbox," when one is ignoring the other's space, is often a non-threatening way to be reminded of boundary reverence.

THE DECISION

The Decision ... When the time comes to make The Decision, write an honest assessment of your relationship. Are there any warning bells? (Ignoring them will *not* make them go away.)

Refer back to the attributes listed in "Marriage Criteria," Decision Section to determine your priorities.... After you have gathered *your* Prince's necessary requirements and sufficiently queried your friends and relatives, let your pen go until it stops. Wait for a while to be sure that nothing further wants to be written. Then, seek quiet time with your inner voice. LISTEN to what she has to say. Although others may have sound advice, your inner voice *knows* best. Not only is she the one *most* invested in your well-being, she is the *only* one who has witnessed *everything* (your thoughts, your feelings, your behaviors, his behaviors) from the beginning. GOOD LUCK!

If he is your Prince ... get serious about tackling the premarital issues that need to be discussed with him.

If he is a Toad ... grit your teeth and get ready to bear the pain.

There are 2 ways to break up:

1. "Cold turkey," in which you completely sever the relationship.
2. "Weaning," in which you continue some form of contact until you feel ready to let each other go.

Each approach has its advantages and disadvantages. Let your intuition advise you regarding which way will be most effective for you. If you are breaking up with someone in which some level of continued contact is necessary (mutual children or friends), strive to get to the point where you no longer feel "stirred up,"(sexually attracted, anger, hatred, sad, hurt) in his presence.

What if "a good man" wants me and I don't want him? ... As soon as you know that he is not your Prince, begin the process of terminating the relationship. You are doing him a disservice if you continue to stay in the relationship after you have made up your mind that he is not your selection. He is going to hurt regardless of when you do it. The longer you wait the more painful it will be for both of you. Practice the rules of "tactful rejection" (see exercise, Hunt section) by ending the relationship in the way in which *you* would want someone to close with you. Remember to remain kind, respectful, and tactful.

"Remaining friends"... after a break up (whether he is a Toad or a "good man") is usually quite unrealistic. Occasionally, with the passing of time, a friendship may be resumed.

COMMITMENT AND MARRIAGE

Keeping the Marriage interesting ... Commit that at least once a week you will do something to keep the marriage enticing.

"Continuing Education" ... Incorporate into your marriage designated times of the year to seek out and *follow through* with "Continuing Education."

Recreation Time ... If you don't make it a priority it won't happen! Set realistic goals with your mate for individual, couple, family, and social time. (See "Continuing Education and Recreation Time," Commitment and Marriage Section for explanation of these terms.)

Hidden Agendas and Expectations ... During one of your regular "check-ins," allot enough time to brainstorm how many marriage myths you can name. Exposing these myths may help you dismiss them. Designate future "check-ins" to discuss (not fight about) hidden agendas and expectations in your marriage.

Forgiving a Partner ... If you are having difficulty forgiving your partner, propose an appointment time in which you will share all your past hurts with him.

If he agrees, on your own, write down everything you can remember, spanning the entire relationship, that has been painful. At the designated hour, read your list to him. He needs to consent that his role will be to look at you while you are speaking and when you are finished, say: "Thank you" and give you a hug. He is *not* allowed to clarify or defend any of the items on the list. If you are not up to sharing your hurts out loud, put them in a letter. How he responds to the exercise (sharing in person or writing the letter) may give you some clues regarding the next step in this relationship.

This assignment may be expanded into one in which you *both* make up lists and, at the appointed time share your items with each other. The purpose of this task is twofold:

1. To express hurt feelings that the other may not even know about, in an environment in which you have agreed to give each other your full attention.

2. To negotiate which items you are each prepared to "discard" and which need further discussion.

Self Generated Exercises ... Create your own exercises based on the particular issues which are challenging you. Be patient with yourself, don't give up, and above all, practice, practice, practice!

SEEKING PROFESSIONAL HELP

How do you know ... if psychotherapy is a wise option for you? M. Scott Peck, M.D. has a simple answer:

> *"When you're stuck"*
> The Road Less Traveled & Beyond

GENERAL GUIDELINES:

1. **Take the choice seriously....** It may be one of the most important decisions you ever make. It has been continuously demonstrated that the RELATIONSHIP between the therapist and the client is a major determinant across various theoretical orientations (psychodynamic, behavioral, cognitive, gestalt, humanistic, existential) regarding successful psychotherapy outcome. (Note that successful psychotherapy outcome is defined by the *client's* self report of considering herself healed.)

2. **The purpose of the first session** ... is as much for *you* to interview the therapist as it is for the therapist to interview you.

3. **Before you begin the "Therapist Hunt"** ... spend some quiet time noticing whether the gender of the therapist is an important factor for you. What personality characteristics would be most appealing to you? Sometimes it is easier to figure out what you *don't* want.

4. **If your state requires licensing** ... be sure to select a licensed practitioner.

5. **Word of mouth** ... is an excellent way to begin the search. If you have a friend who has had a successful experience, either

start with that therapist or get a referral from him/her. If you do not know anyone who has had a successful experience, call a local doctors' referral center or a national mental health organization such as the American Psychiatric Association,

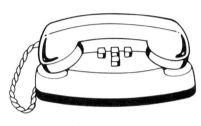

American Psychological Association, or the American Association for Marriage & Family Therapy. The yellow pages should be a last resort.

6. **It is a good idea ...** to do therapist shopping. You have a better idea of what you are looking for when you have interviewed a few therapists.

7. **When you meet the therapist ...** notice whether your inner voice is speaking and/or what messages your body is sending you. These cues are providing you with the data to determine whether the therapist is genuine, caring, honest, ethical, and competent. He/she may be all of the above, but if you do not feel safe and comfortable or trust that this person will make your well-being paramount ... move on.

8. **Pay more attention ...** to your "gut" than to the "three letters" after his/her name.

9. **If you sense ...** that he/she will provide treatment to anyone, proceed to your next prospect. An ethical and competent psychotherapist knows that he/she is not a good match for *every* person who comes through the front door. He/she also knows that some clients are beyond his/her realm of expertise.

10. **If you are wondering ...** about his/her position with regard to certain issues such as abortion, spirituality, feminism, or

homosexuality, ask. If he/she is not interested in telling you, move on.

11. **If you do not have insurance ...** go to a mental health clinic or a nonprofit agency such as the United Way. Their charge is based on income level. Sometimes an independent practitioner will see clients on a lower fee schedule. You have lost nothing if you ask the question. If you participate in a managed care program, it does not mean that you have no choice with regard to practitioner. It means that you must exhibit more perseverance.

Entering psychotherapy is a very courageous act ... because the process involves "killing off" old habits and beliefs in order to provide s p a c e for the new. Reconstruction of a familiar and long-standing blueprint is tedious, stressful, and demanding. The journey is difficult, exhausting, and frightening. However, in spite of all its challenging components, a *successful* psychotherapeutic experience is transforming and one of the most inspirational pilgrimages of this life.

ABOUT THE AUTHOR

Dr. Tobler is a clinical psychologist. She maintained a large independent practice (specializing in couples psychotherapy) in the Washington, D.C. area from 1976 to 1994. In 1994 she relocated to Southwest Florida to devote a portion of her career to writing. She is a clinical member of AAMFT (American Association for Marriage and Family Therapy), and a certified PAIRS (Practical Application of Intimate Relationship Skills) Leader. PAIRS is an internationally known program dedicated to teaching the necessary skills to create and maintain satisfying, healthy, and loving relationships.

Additional copies of this book are available at:

AMAZON.COM

BARNES & NOBLE.COM

For immediate assistance you may call:

PERIWINKLE PRESS at:

1-888-411-TOAD